A Faithful Past, A Shining Future

75 Years of Pentecostal Education at North Central University

Minneapolis, Minnesota

A Faithful Past, A Shining Future

75 Years of Pentecostal Education
at North Central University

ISBN 0-9762461-2-0
Library of Congress Number 2006901943

Printed in the U.S.A. by
Morris Publishing
3212 East Highway 30
Kearney, NE 68847
1-800-650-7888

Published by
North Central University Press
910 Elliot Ave.
Minneapolis, MN 55404
1.800.289.6222
www.northcentral.edu

A Faithful Past, A Shining Future:
75 Years of Pentecostal Education at North Central University
© 2006 by North Central University

All rights reserved. No part of this book may be reproduced in any form except for the inclusion of brief quotations in a review, without permission in writing from the publisher.

Photos included in this book are the property of North Central University, used by permission.

Acknowledgements

Thank you to the editorial team, comprised of students, faculty and staff, who worked diligently to put this book together:

Hope Bahr
Lafe Blobaum
Susan Detlefsen
Joanne Kersten
Jonathon Porter
Amy Sturgeon
Dr. Carolyn Tennant
NCU Administration
and the many North Central Alumni who donated their time, talents and resources.

A note from the editorial team: The purpose of this book is to capture memories and events of North Central Bible Institute, Bible College, and University that have shaped thousands of lives during the last 75 years. It is not intended to be an exhaustive account of the history of the institution, but mainly a memory book. The editorial team acknowledges the efforts and lives of hundreds of people who may not be mentioned in the following pages, but have made an indelible mark on the institution just the same. To those who have been willing to serve, and to the many who still do, thank you.

The alumni essays that are printed in this book were edited for size. Unedited versions of these manuscripts, including some additional materials, have been submitted as permanent records in NCU Archives housed in the T.J. Jones Information Resource Center. Thank you to the many alumni who generously shared their stories.

"North Central Bible College happened in 1930. It was no accident. It was born of God because people everywhere were searching for answers to the hunger of their souls. God heard them praying. He gave them the answer by inspiring the North Central idea... 'Training young people for world-wide ministries.'"
– D. H. Mapson, Director of Development, 1970

"An illuminated mind which appreciates spiritual values is the best vehicle which God can secure....Time is too short for delay. We cannot wait until our education is completed to begin winning men for Christ. We are the 'light of the world' and our responsibility is to let the light of our testimony shine forth into a sin-darkened world before it is too late."
– 1944 Yearbook

"The training of young people for Christian service is truly a God-ordained and highly important ministry."
– 1946 *Archive* Yearbook

Contents

Foreword 9
by General Superintendent Thomas E. Trask

Baptized with Pentecostal Flame 11
by Heather Owen

Chapter 1 13
History from 1930-1954

Chapter 2 27
Alumni memories from 1930-1954

Chapter 3 73
History from 1955-1979

Chapter 4 89
Alumni memories from 1955-1979

Chapter 5 117
History from 1980-2005

Chapter 6 137
Alumni memories from 1980-2005

Chapter 7 183
Selected photography

Afterword 193
by President Gordon Anderson

Foreword

Who would have ever dreamed when North Central Bible Institute was begun 75 years ago, as a result of the vision and passion of Frank J. Lindquist, that from a small beginning ("For who hath despised the day of small things" Zechariah 4:10) would today be an incredible army that is spread around the world changing their world through the power of the Gospel of Jesus Christ. To God be the glory!

My introduction to North Central came when my father, who was a presbyter of the Minnesota District, said, "You're going to Bible school." That came as a complete surprise for me. You see, I was not serving the Lord at the time. I was enjoying high school, playing basketball and running track. My response was, "Not me!" Dad said, "Yes, you are for I have already enrolled you." I went, against my will, but it was during the first semester of my freshman year that a revival broke out and classes were suspended for days. It was on the floor in the old chapel behind the elevator of the original building that God overhauled this preacher's kid and placed the call of God upon my life. I was never to be the same.

I shall be eternally grateful for the instructors that helped shape my life, men and women such as T. J. Jones (I used to take him to the train depot every Friday as he left Minneapolis for weekend ministry and then pick him up on Monday morning in time for his classes), Ione Soltau, John Phillipps, Ray Levang, Ivan O. Miller, Harold Tangmo, Marvin Nelson, and many, many more.

It was at North Central I met my wife of 49 years who had gone to Bible school to prepare to serve the Lord. From this union four beautiful children were born who are serving the Lord in Christian service today. Our oldest son, Brad, is a second generation graduate of North Central Bible College. I owe so very much to this institution and for the tremendous blessing it has been to our lives.

I am thrilled at the great contribution it is making to the Fellowship known as the Assemblies of God. It has and continues to send forth pastors, associate pastors, missionaries, evangelists, teachers, and Spirit-filled lay people who bless this church in immeasurable ways. I want to say thank you to President Gordon Anderson, faculty, staff, and administration for the sterling leadership that is being provided through North Central University. The development of the campus is a testimony of one miracle after another. God uses men and women who believe in this school's mission of providing Pentecostal integration of Christian higher education to send forth men and women in the power of the Holy Spirit. With as rich a history as North Central has, I believe the days ahead, should the Lord tarry, have never been brighter.

We say thank you to all who have served and are serving and will serve.

Thomas E. Trask
General Superintendent of the Assemblies of God
NCBC Alumnus, Class of 1956

Baptized with Pentecostal Flame

Fifteen and threescore years have passed, The plan of God unfolding!
A thousand lives each year go through the processes of moulding.
Then "Vessels unto Honor" formed by loving nail-scarred Hands
Are used in God's great Kingdom here at home and foreign lands.
To teach God's Word with power is the vision that they had,
It started in the Chapel of the Lake Street "Gospel Tab"
Frank Lindquist and his wife, Irene, with those in teaching, skilled
Met there each day and found indeed! their vision was fulfilled!
The students kept on coming until enrollment grew,
Crowding out the Chapel, by filling every pew!
And then the Lord provided in His Providential care
A Hospital that was for sale with lots of room in there
But I'll not dwell on buildings and the way the Lord provided
I'm more concerned with what they learned, The Truth, "rightly divided"
All through the years, 'mid toil and tears, financial burdens too,
Our faith has never faltered and we proved that 'God came through'
"Jesus' Blood, we magnify, His empty tomb our battle cry.
Our fortress strong, His mighty Name, Our 'blazoned sign His Cross of shame.'
Baptized with Pentecostal Flame.
We march to victory!"

by Heather Owen
NCBC music teacher, and wife of David Owen,
Welsh pastor, evangelist, and professor at NCBC

Chapter One

Historical Review 1930-1954

Researched and written by Lafe Blobaum, Class of 2005

"You must begin a Bible school."

It was 1929 when Lillian B. Yeomans boldly spoke those prophetic words to the superintendent of the North Central District of the Assemblies of God. "Your young people need the training they can only get in a Bible school," Yeomans told F.J. Lindquist. Though Lindquist's immediate response to this brazen proclamation is unknown, a seed was planted. As the pastor of the Minneapolis Gospel Tabernacle, Lindquist had already found the importance of Biblical knowledge to be true in his own life. He believed in the benefit of ministerial training, having taken some correspondence courses through Moody Bible Institute. "I knew how important it was that ministers be able to study the Word of God," Lindquist said. "So often, in the early days, the average Pentecostal preacher had the idea that he could open his mouth and the Lord would fill it."

All of this came to life in the fall of 1930 when North Central Bible Institute's first classes were held in the basement of Lindquist's church. More than 30 students from throughout the North Central District descended upon Minneapolis to pursue the call of God upon their lives. Along with regular day sessions, the Institute also offered evening classes in its inaugural year, which drew an additional 80 students. Like today, the night school provided a learning opportunity for non-traditional students. Many of the night school students were adult members of Minneapolis Gospel Tabernacle who wanted a stronger foundation in Bible teaching.

Highlights of the first year included visits by several guest ministers. Among them were Charles Price, J.N. Hoover, Willard Pierce, and Lillian B. Yeomans, who were no doubt pleased to see the immediate success of Lindquist's Bible school.

The curriculum set up by Lindquist and his staff was designed to be a three-year program. As a result, in its first year, the school had only one group of students. The student body more than doubled the following year, however, with over 30 new students beginning their first year, and 22 of the original 26 returning for the second. As the school outgrew the basement, they improvised, moving classes to the church's balcony. Though the Tabernacle was still under construction, the congregation served as gracious hosts to the Institute during its first few years.

The Second Year

As NCBI expanded, Lindquist, acting as President, initiated changes to accommodate the growth. These changes included hiring a larger staff. For the 1931-1932 school year, Charles Beatty served as Vice President and later as Dean of Students. Ruth Campbell stepped in as Dean of Women, and James T. Paulos was the Music Director. The faculty that year was comprised of three women – Ruth E. Osgood, Ruth J. McLeod, and Lillian B. Yeomans.

Having been given the first year to fine tune things, the administration outlined a more structured class schedule in the 1931-

1932 catalog. The school year was composed of three terms, and courses taught covered five major disciplines – general Bible study, Christian ministry, missions, Christian education, and music.

The students' spiritually rigorous school days began at 8 a.m. The first 45 minutes of the day served as a time to focus on God through corporate prayer, worship, and a message from a teacher or student. As the day went on, prayer and singing at the beginning of each class period helped students maintain this focus. In addition, 30 minutes of prayer was reserved at lunchtime to pray for homework and for missionaries and their work in the foreign fields. The 1931-32 school year also saw the birth of North Central's first student newspaper, *The Northcentralian*, and an orchestra, boasting 12 members in its first year.

The 1932-33 school year was a landmark year as NCBI honored its first graduates. "If the Lord tarries, I am sure the institute will outgrow its present quarters in the Minneapolis Gospel Tabernacle. It makes us very happy, that a class of 19 students will graduate this year," Lindquist is quoted in the 1933 yearbook.

Out of the 33 who had started in October 1930, 19 students finished the three-year program. This charter class, having been immersed in studies, prayer, and practical ministry, was ready to step into the ministry God had prepared for them. Graduating classes in the following years continued to grow, with 25 students finishing in 1934, 39 in 1935, and 45 in 1936.

Journal Entry

The following is a page from the 1934 yearbook entitled "From a Senior's Diary."

1933

September 25 – Back again. We have left our homes and our various occupations and now we are once more in

Bible School. Around us we see many of our old friends and a host of new ones.

26 – We had a treat today. Mr. Sidusky, a converted Jew, dramatized for us an orthodox Jewish Passover.

30 – Tonight the Christ Ambassadors of the Minneapolis Tabernacle gave us our annual reception.

October 2 – It is now time to get down to business. This morning Brother Olson gave out the assignments for Practical Work.

31 – This was a day of outpouring of the Holy Spirit. The freshmen started praying during the first hour; the other classes joined them at recess, and "My, did it rain!"

November 19 – The China Mission Band presented the first program.

24 – This Friday we endeavored to kill two birds with one stone. We had our annual Thanksgiving dinner and celebrated President Lindquist's Birthday.

29 – Left school for our first vacation. It lasted four days.

December 19 – The school gave its annual Christmas program.

22 – Our first term is safely over, and we are going home for the holidays, which will last from December 22 to January 2.

1934

January 2 – The second term began today. "Present in body, but absent in spirit."

28 – South American Missionary program.

30 – A number of valuable books were added to the library.

February 6 – The freshmen began leading chapel. The seniors are composing music.

21, 22, 23 – Three days of special prayer.

Chapter One

March 9 – We enter into the last lap of the race (third term).

12 – "Emancipation Day" for the seniors.

16 – The boys gathered at Powderhorn Park and played ball, and of course –

17 – Complaints of sore arms and sorer legs.

19 – Heart stirring pictures of the tribulation in Russia were shown by Brother Patmont.

April 3 – The annual *Archive*-selling contest began.

14 – The Juniors gave the seniors their annual banquet. Plenty to eat and a good time for all.

May 11 – The student body enjoyed the annual picnic at Powderhorn. It didn't rain.

13 – President Lindquist preached the Baccalaureate sermon. I know we'll miss his splendid messages after we leave.

14 – Class Day and Program at night.

15 – COMMENCEMENT

16 – School is out. Good-bye and hope we'll see you again soon!

Student Housing

The absence of student housing during NCBI's years at the Tabernacle forced many students to work harder to find a place to live while in school. In many ways, women were at an advantage because of the culture of the 1930's. At that time, it was relatively easy for a young lady to receive room and board in a Minneapolis home in exchange for cooking and cleaning duties. Men, however, were not so fortunate. Many had to work long hours to cover living expenses (about $7 per week), and often shared apartments with other male students. School administration was aware of these difficulties and offered help to the students. They played a part in placing the young women in welcoming homes and connecting the young men with businesses in need of help. At times, however, this was a lengthy process. Irene Lindquist recalls that at one point, she and Frank were housing 13 students in the basement of their parsonage. This shows further evidence of the tight-knit family that was NCBI during its early years.

A New Home

As the class sizes began to balloon, Lindquist started searching for a new home for NCBI. The school had been strapped for space ever since the beginning, but they had made it work. By 1936, it was obvious that something must be done. Lindquist and Ivan O. Miller were scouting out buildings on a cold winter day when they came to 910 Elliot Avenue. The massive brick building they stumbled upon had once housed Asbury Methodist Hospital, but now stood deserted. Above the front entrance was an engraving that caught the men's attention. "Not to be ministered unto, but to minister." This had been the hospital's motto, and seemed appropriate for their dreams as well. Though it was in desperate need of repair, Lindquist and Miller wanted this building to be NCBI's new home.

Upon seeing the building that day, Lindquist set out on a crusade to purchase the old hospital for NCBI. His research uncovered that the five-story structure, valued at nearly $470,000, was being offered by the Board of Asbury Hospital for $500,000, with a one percent down payment. NCBI's bank account held only $100. Lindquist set out for Springfield to obtain a gift or loan for $5,000 to cover the down payment. This was a request the Executive Presbytery could not grant. With the nation slowly recovering from the Great Depression, no one seemed to have money. A dejected Lindquist returned to tell the hospital board of his failure to find money for a down payment. In a move that no doubt shocked Lindquist, the Hospital Board offered to lend NCBI the money for the down payment. As further proof of God's work in the situation, Lindquist was able to negotiate the price down to $125,000.

Chapter One

With this ammunition, Lindquist returned to the Institute's Board of Directors and the North Central District Presbytery for their approval. Though they all knew that the building was a bargain, $125,000 was still more money than most could fathom. After numerous visits to the property, and to God's throne in prayer, the proposal was approved and the building was purchased.

There were many repairs to be made. Lindquist petitioned all churches in the North Central District to give as much money as they were able toward renovations. The new home needed to be ready for the upcoming school year starting September 20, 1937. Ariel Henders LeRoy (class of 1938) remembered, "The students became excited about the new – old deserted building and many worked all summer to clean and repair it, including Frank and I. With support from the churches, and hard work by both students and faculty, the building was ready that fall. NCBI could now feed and house its own students, up to 225 of them."

Ruth (Rector) Olsen, a member of the third graduating class of North Central, and other students walked from the Gospel Tabernacle on Lake Street down to the Asbury Hospital on Elliot Park. They worked for days cleaning the building so that it could be occupied.

The Asbury Hospital acquisition was probably the most important event in North Central's first 25 years. The school now had a building to call its own. And it wasn't just any average building. Its description in a 1938 NCBI publication gives us an idea of the pride that the school showed in its new home:

"One full city block in length. Five stories high. Newly decorated throughout. Absolutely fireproof in construction. No fire worries in classroom or in your bed at night. Spacious, well-lighted classrooms both for Bible School and Business College. Large, comfortably seated chapel. Beautifully furnished, comfortable, well-lighted dormitory rooms. Elevator service. Ventilating system. Cafeteria. Confectionery. Laundry. One of the finest Bible School buildings in

America. Replacement valuation over $1 million."

Practical Work

North Central has never simply focused on classroom learning. Students during the first 25 years took what they learned in classes out into the community. Maintaining a balance between hands-on ministry experience and academics was a difficult challenge then as it is now. Students of that time were often involved in ministry two or three times each week, as they are now.

Aware that ministry opportunities abounded in the Twin Cities, the Practical Work department existed to keep students involved in local evangelism. In addition to attending Friday and Sunday services at the Minneapolis Gospel Tabernacle, students were required to participate in some other type of ministry. The practical work groups started Bible studies in area homes, led evangelistic meetings, taught Sunday school, distributed tracts, and played musical specials.

One product of the Practical Work department was Glad Tidings Chapel. This mission, tagged as a "soul-saving station," was located on Nicollet Avenue, a half block south of Lake Street. It was operated entirely by students. During the school year, young people led music and preached at Glad Tidings five nights each week, as well as on Sunday afternoons.

For many years, W. A. Katter oversaw the Practical Work department. A few churches pioneered through the work of NCBI students include Northfield Gospel Chapel, Stillwater Assembly of God, Bloomington Assembly of God and City of Lakes Church, which Katter left to pastor full-time in 1949. D.V. Hurst assumed Katter's position, and continued to make the Practical Work department one of NCBI's most active student departments. Other Practical Work leaders in the first 25 years include Paul Wilson and Arvid Kingsriter. By 1955, the department was involved in over 50 ministry endeavors, covering a 100-mile radius.

Chapter One

Missionary Bands

North Central's international focus was also evident from the start. All students were assigned to teams, called Missionary Bands, which met each Friday afternoon to work on special projects. During this time, the bands researched particular regions of the world and prepared presentations to share with the entire student body. Often times, the bands also shared their findings with the Tabernacle's youth group. These groups were not only informative for the listeners, but also impacted the students conducting the research. Though North Central's missions major was not developed until later, many NCBI graduates during these years answered a call to the foreign fields after graduating.

As the years passed, meeting times changed, but the Missionary Bands remained intact throughout the first 25 years. They grew from six bands in 1933, to 12 in 1954. For many years, these were the primary student organizations on campus. They elected officers, held regular meetings, and sponsored events that raised missions awareness and money for missionaries in their specific regions. Along with these fundraisers was the annual Missions Pledge Offering, which began in the mid 1930's and has continued ever since.

Academic Programs

In 1938, in a move to serve a greater variety of students, administration made plans to start a business college. The mission of North Central Business College (NCBC) was to train young men and women in skills demanded by the business industry of that time. Typing, shorthand, accounting, and business English were all taught in the classrooms. NCBI's pitch was "Enroll Any Monday." The coursework was designed so that students could begin classes at any time during the school year. As a result, many students came and went throughout the year. During its existence, Ivan O. Miller served as Dean of both NCBI and NCBC, but the business college was short-lived, and was not offered after 1945.

Music has always been an important part of NCBI. An excerpt from an early NCBI catalog reads, "The ministry of music is second only to that of preaching." Starting with the first orchestra in 1932, North Central students were active in music in the church and in the classroom. Though musical study was always an option for students, a huge step was taken in 1946. This was the year that NCBI teamed up with the Minneapolis-based MacPhail School of Music. With this new partnership, students could complete the three-year NCBI music program, then finish a fourth year of study at MacPhail to earn a Bachelor of Music degree.

The MacPhail partnership was not the institute's only cooperative endeavor. NCBI worked hard to help students with interests outside the majors offered. During the 1940's, administration worked with the University of Minnesota to allow students to earn credit for courses taken there. With the exception of the school of business, NCBI did not offer any traditional non-ministry majors at this time.

NCBI expanded its course offering in 1945, allowing young people a choice of four courses of study. The theology course was a continuation of NCBI's general Bible studies, but students could also enroll in the missionary, music, or Christian education course. In the missionary course, students received in-depth teaching of the theology of missions and missionary strategies. The music program was designed for those with the desire to be worship leaders. Finally, those who chose the Christian education course learned various aspects of church leadership – secretarial skills, child evangelism, and music theory.

In the fall of 1946, administration was happy to introduce a four-year degree to NCBI's program. Months earlier, Lindquist and other school officials had met with the General Council of Bible Schools in Springfield, Missouri. In those meetings, they discussed what must be done to add a bachelor's degree to NCBI's offerings. Quick

Chapter One

changes were made, and the 1946 catalog included a bachelor's degree in Religious Education. Unfortunately, the program did not last, and NCBI stopped offering four-year degrees in 1949.

When NCBI began in the wake of the depression, money was tight and tuition was cheap. In 1931, the school charged $51 for one year's tuition. This cost included books, but not room or board. When NCBI relocated and was able to house and feed its students, it charged an all-inclusive fee of $160. This bargain price, however, was conditional upon the students helping out on campus 10 hours each week.

Other Student Activities

As NCBI grew each year, so did its plethora of student activities. Because many students were unable to return home for the short Thanksgiving weekend, the school celebrated as any family did. A feast was prepared for all students and faculty. This dinner conveniently coincided with President Lindquist's birthday, November 26, and was always included in the festivities. Another regular get-together was the end of the year picnic at Powderhorn Park. This was fitting because of NCBI's proximity to the park, but continued even after the school moved to the Elliot Park neighborhood.

The Northcentralian, the school's original newspaper, eventually evolved into a bimonthly alumni publication and was printed for many years. With *The Northcentralian* as their primary communication, leaders launched the NCBI Alumni Association in 1934. This was an important move that helped the school track the progress of graduates who now traveled all over the globe. A new student newspaper, *The Scroll* was started in 1943. In 1946, its name changed to the *Archette*, which stuck for years to come. Student Council has also been around since the beginning. Representatives from each class met regularly to discuss problems, pray, and propose solutions.

Name Changes

Lindquist served as the superintendent of the Assemblies of God's North Central District, and it seemed appropriate for the school to bear its name. The North Central District was always the primary source for students. There were, however, tweaks to the institution's name over the years. When administration added the business college, NCBI-NCBC became the hyphenated alternative. This, of course, was dropped when the business program folded in 1945. In 1946, the bachelor of arts degree in Religious Education showed up in the catalog, and officials added Theological Seminary to the school's tag, making it NCBI&TS. But in 1949, when the degree was discontinued, Theological Seminary left school's name, bringing them back where they started, North Central Bible Institute.

The First 25 Years Close

At the end of NCBI's 25th year, it had graduated 1,423 graduates. Fifty had served as missionaries on foreign fields and 10 had been NCBI faculty members. Sixty percent of graduates were active in professional ministry.

Staff and Administration

Founder and longtime president Frank J. Lindquist served faithfully at NCBI throughout its first quarter-century and into the second. From lending his church building in NCBI's earliest stages, to spearheading the move to its current home on Elliot Avenue, to overseeing the growth of its academic programs – Lindquist's bold vision and blind faith will not be forgotten.

Library namesake T.J. Jones joined the teaching staff at NCBI in the fall of 1946. It wasn't long before Jones was promoted to Principal, and later Dean of Students. A native of England, Jones left a legacy at NCBI as a great Bible teacher and expositor.

Chapter One

Ivan O. Miller is another man who saw NCBI through many changes. Miller's testimony includes being miraculously healed of tuberculosis and fighting in the First World War. Once the pastor of Brainerd Gospel Tabernacle, the assistant superintendent of the North Central District came on board as Dean of NCBI in 1936. Miller retained this position until 1945, when he was promoted to Vice President of NCBI.

Another man who served as Dean in NCBI's first 25 years is Emil Balliet. At one time the choir director and assistant pastor of the Minneapolis Gospel Tabernacle, Balliet taught music and Bible at NCBI from 1935 to 1944. In 1944, he stepped in as Dean of Students for one year, and Principal for two years.

Many loved a product of NCBI's charter class, Anna Froland Magnuson, when she served as Dean of Women from 1936 to 1945. Other notable faculty include alum John P. Phillipps and former District Superintendent G. Raymond Carlson, who both began lengthy teaching careers at NCBI in 1948.

Rules

The following are rules included in course catalogs from the first 25 years:

- Pupils are not allowed to enter into any engagement to be married while in school.
- Men students are not allowed to go out with any women or to call upon any woman without permission from the Dean. If the woman to be visited is a student, permission must also be obtained from the Supervisor of Women.
- Students must not visit a home or outside place without permission from the Dean; women from the Supervisor of Women.
- Young men and young women are not permitted to go out together over any week-end, holiday or during any school vacation.
- Students who are owners of cars must use them consistently

in the light of the school regulations or have that privilege taken from them by the Faculty.

- Students are admonished not to wear necklaces or to use rouge or lipstick.
- Students will be allowed to sit together at tables in the dining room during meal hours. The same couple will not be allowed to sit together more than once each day.
- Men or women who desire to correspond with men or women other than their own immediate relatives must obtain permission.
- No food may be taken to the rooms without permission from some Faculty Member.
- Students are forbidden to attend any meetings in other churches than their own without special individual permission from the Dean.

Chapter Two

Alumni Memories 1930-1954

Learning To Know God as Provider

Anna Olson Edson
Class of 1936

My first experience with NCU was 1934, very near its beginning. I was a new Christian, having come to the Lord at Minneapolis Gospel Tabernacle. Since the Bible School was located at the Tabernacle, I was not quite sure which was the Bible school and which was church.

During my senior year I met a girl who also attended high school on the north side of the city and had a strong faith in Christ. She helped me immensely in my Christian walk.

In my eleventh year of high school, I supported myself by working for room and board at $2 per week and by faith. I learned about tithing; with 20 cents at least going to the church. I needed streetcar fare two to three times per week plus clothing and other normal needs. Somehow, I got by financially. Financial pressures were common, with most young women working in private homes after attending morning classes.

Fridays were special. We girls could wear bright and ruffled collars on our black uniforms and share our noon lunches with young men.

In order to avoid graduation expenses, I decided to request my diploma without participating in graduation ceremonies. God had a better plan. He provided a complete new graduation outfit, a hairdo at the beauty parlor, new shoes, a new dress, and dinner at the home of the Mayor of Minneapolis, complete with a ride to the ceremony in the Mayor's limousine.

After graduation, I spent some very interesting years in Sheldon, Wisconsin. My friend, Agnes Rawdon, and I hitchhiked to Lake Geneva Bible Camp. It is there that God brought Donald (class of 1938) and I together over 67 years ago. In 1940, we married, and in 2006 we will have been married for 66 years.

We are extremely grateful for the part that NCBI has had in our lives, as we watched it grow from a fledgling Bible school to an accredited Bible college, and now university.

Before Us Lies the Timber! Let Us Build!

Donald Edson
Class of 1938

After becoming a Christian in the Bismarck Assembly of God Church, I felt the call of God on my life to attend Bible school to become a minister. Pastor Marvin Miller, brother of Ivan Miller, counseled me toward North Central. At the age of 23, in 1936, I arrived at NCBI, I then housed at 13th and Lake at Minneapolis Gospel Tabernacle. I made it through the three-year course in two years, graduating in 1938. I was one of the speakers at my own graduation program. By then the school had moved into Miller Hall, the business college had been launched, and I began studying business.

That summer I met Anna Marie Olson at Lake Geneva Bible Camp. After knowing her four days, I asked her to marry me. She said, "Yes", and we have been married 65-plus years. Because of my previous education as a teacher and my NCU education, I was made a teacher at the business college, where I taught for 10 years. The 1949 and 1950 *Archive* [yearbooks] show me as the Dean of Men and teacher of many different subjects. Around the same time, I began pastoring churches that include Cambridge Gospel Tabernacle, 48th Street Christian Church, and Columbia Heights Assembly of God.

Some of the students I taught during those years went on to have significant ministries. A few of those students include: John Phillipps, who taught at North Central for 30 years; Duane Hurst, who taught at NCU and later became president of Northwest College in Kirkland, Washington; Monroe and Betty Jane Haas Grams, who were missionaries in South and Central America for 45 years.

Anna and I have deeply appreciated the experience and influence North Central has had on our lives.

Students and faculty valued writing, art and poetry as evidenced in a school publication known as *The Northcentralian*. The April 1936, Vol. V, No. 4 issue included the Commencement Program of May 12, 1936, including articles, poetry, and stories by Norma Ojala, George Skaret, Evelyn Westlund, and a song by Kenneth Olson, Paul Hild, Frances Axtell.

Class motto: Before us lies the timber! Let us Build!

Business Skills Essential for My Ministry

Elizabeth Abbott
based on an interview by Dr. Carolyn Tennant, Feb. 2005

Catherine Searles Hanson attended the North Central Business

Institute between 1938-1940. For Catherine, North Central Business College was essential and timely. God's design prepared her for a field of labor in the corporate business world.

"God needs witnesses in each sector of the world," stressed Catherine Searles Hanson. "I used the business training I received at NCBI every day of my life personally, in corporate business, and in the churches in which I was attending. I simply could not have worked effectively for the Lord without the knowledge gleaned from my NCBI education. In fact, I am still busy using it for the Lord!"

Those friends in the Waupaca, Wisconsin area in which Catherine resides can validate the quickness of mind, freshness of heart, and witty spirit that characterizes her to this present day.

Elizabeth Abbott says she grew up poor in Fargo during the depression. Five of her six siblings ended up in the ministry. She always desired to be a preacher's wife and remembers at 21 praying in the Fargo Assemblies of God Church and feeling that she should go to Bible school. She came in the summer of 1941 when the General Council met in Minneapolis.

Elizabeth got a job working for 25 cents per hour for Tommy Griffith, the Registrar, and also in the cafeteria. She remembers that very few had cars and had to walk a long way to their jobs. "Some might laugh at our uniforms," said Elizabeth, "but I liked them. None of us had too many clothes, and we didn't have to worry about what we were going to wear. I had one black one. The choir usually sang at the Tab [now Christ's Church], but we were excused from wearing our uniform if it was at the cleaner's."

Elizabeth's future husband, Bob, came to North Central because of the influence of Arvid Kingsriter, who took him out after their quartet sang at a church service where Bob was in attendance. He roomed with Ken Freiheit, long-time secretary-treasurer of the Minnesota District. Wes Hurst ultimately asked Bob himself to sing in the Gospel Broadcasters, an a cappella group.

Chapter Two

When they were in school, Elizabeth recalled that freshmen could have one date every two weeks, juniors could have one date every week, and seniors could have two dates per week…only these had to be pre-approved with a permission slip from the Dean of Men or Women. "I remember he came up to me and said, 'Liz, how about a date tonight?" That turned into 55 years of marriage! They married the day after Elizabeth graduated.

From 1943 to 1969 the Abbotts pastored in various towns in Minnesota including Emily, Two Harbors, Thief River Falls, Alexandria, and Little Falls. In 1969 they became evangelists. Elizabeth recalls that they didn't know what to do as evangelists. God showed them many things, and they began to concentrate on children, utilizing much innovative media for those times. They often stayed in peoples' homes and lived on the road. They maintained a strong schedule of ministry on the road, traveling right up to the time that Bob passed away in 1999.

"I have never been sorry that I chose North Central," said Elizabeth with enthusiasm and energy. She remembers times of prayer when God moved and classes were cancelled. She says she received the flow of tongues and the fullness of the Holy Spirit at North Central. Elizabeth still comes back often to visit her alma mater and has many wonderful stories about her time at NCBI and the ministry that the Lord gave her and her husband, Bob.

Haven't Stopped Preaching Since Then

David Flower
based on an interview by Dr. Carolyn Tennant, Feb. 2005

David Flower was president of the Freshman Class in 1942-43. He recalls holding down two jobs. In the evening he served as the bell hop at what was then the Vendome Hotel, and when he got off work at midnight, he went to a restaurant to clean it up. In between he managed to attend classes and make some friends. In fact, he says he still maintains some of those friendships. Flower lived on the fourth floor of what is now Miller Hall in a room that housed five including Bud Abbott, David Schrepple, and Oral Krans. David was also a member of King's Ambassadors, a trio which started on their own and then got busy, so the school decided to sponsor them.

Some of the students were on a semi-pro basketball team which included David, Del Kingsriter and Clarence and Erwin Rohde. When asked where they practiced, David said, "We didn't. We had no suits that matched either. But we actually beat some pretty good teams!" All five of the Rohde brothers greatly touched North Central throughout the years, and contributed so much in various areas, especially in the Midwest, pastoring and serving as district officials.

Flower specifically remembers Emil Balliet as his favorite professor. He eventually became the pastor of Central Assembly of God in Springfield. He remembers that John Phillipps was in the senior class. Phillipps later became a favorite Bible teacher at North Central and has the latest residence hall named after him.

"I preached my first sermon at the Midnight Mission on Hennepin," Flower continued. "I thought that I had notes to last half an hour, but the message only lasted five minutes." His second sermon was at a black church. "I haven't stopped preaching since then," Flower said. His father, J. Roswell Flower, was general secretary of the General Council for many years, and David followed the path of this rich heritage. He went on to pastor in New York, Maine, Massachusetts, Ohio, and was the district superintendent for ten years in Southern New England.

David Flower recalls that the men often prayed down in the boiler room. One night, however, there were twelve of them packed into a room on the south end of third floor. One young man, with his eyes closed the whole time, picked up a Bible and started speaking in tongues. He preached a message in tongues for fifteen minutes. "I will never forget that," said David Flower. "There was a lot of hunger in the freshman class, and it spread throughout the school."

Law, Lordship and Longevity
Bertil O. and Phyllis Thompson Nygaard, class of 1945

Bertil and I began our studies at North Central in the business college. I completed my Biblical studies and business college training in a record two and a half years. After serving in the Navy for over three years, Bert attended the University of Minnesota to receive a bachelor of science degree. After our marriage in 1950, Bertil went on and graduated from William Mitchell Law School in 1954 with a juris doctor degree.

I loved the entire faculty. The Rev. Ivan Miller was a very special and kind person. The Rev. Ted Ness led the Music department very well. Rev. Lindquist was a very strict teacher, but students learned a lot because he expected it from us.

Anna Magnuson Froland was so caring of the girls and placed us in working positions. It was very hard to find jobs in 1941, so she sent me to work in a home in the Lake of the Isles area. This provided room and board and $3.50 per week spending money. I was 17 when I came to attend the business college and had no income except what I could earn. The faculty was very understanding because they, too, had very small incomes.

We learned to trust God for our needs. Much prayer went on in the school. We spent hours in prayer, and I believe that is why so many of my classmates have been so successful for the Lord.

After graduating from NCBI, I went to churches to speak, sing, and conduct vacation Bible schools. I worked in the Rochester Gospel Tabernacle for 10 months, speaking, leading song services and playing the piano.

From 1946 to 1948 I traveled with Norma Dahl in evangelistic meetings throughout Minnesota, South Dakota, Wisconsin and Kansas. The meetings lasted two to three weeks with services every night.

As a practicing lawyer in Golden Valley, Minnesota, Bert did a lot of work for churches under the direction of District Superintendents Stanley Clar, G. Raymond Carlson, and Herman Rohde. Bert incorporated many suburban churches and those throughout the state. He did real estate work and estate planning for hundreds of Christians in the Assemblies of God. He served on the Board of Administration for North Central University, helping them through the regionalization process. He served on the State Board for Campus Crusade and was a board member at Christ's Church for many years.

In 1977, Bert became an Administrative Law Judge for the State of Minnesota. This took him to many cities conducting hearings and appeals. After retiring from law in 1987, Bert enjoyed his family even more, taking trips to Europe and other places.

Bert and I were blessed with two daughters, Jane and Kathryn. Jane is married to Paul Flower, attorney, and has three children named Michael, Mark and Jennifer. Kathryn is working and busy as the leader of a Singles Ministry in her church in Tulsa, Oklahoma, where she is President of the local Toastmaster's Club. My children serve the Lord, which is a great blessing to this octogenarian.

I have enjoyed being involved in God's work ever since my youth. I was a credentialed minister with the Assemblies of God, serving as senior adult ministries director for the Minnesota District for six years. Previous to that I was the Minnesota district director of women's ministries for seven years. Serving as Sunday school teacher,

Bible study leader, president of the Minneapolis Gospel Tabernacle women's missionary council, Minnesota Teen Challenge certified PACE teacher, and current leader of a Park Assembly Bible study and home Bible study with neighborhood friends are some of the activities that I have been committed to in the past years.

What a privilege we have serving the Lord Jesus Christ. I have been truly blessed to have had Bible school training and the support of the Minnesota District Assemblies of God.

Business and Bible In Liberia

Mildred Duncklee Flach

Mildred Duncklee Flach took the Bible and business course at North Central. "Brother Lindquist's messages in chapel were always a blessing!" Professional business knowledge and spiritual inspiration were the tools that brought success and blessing to Mildred.

The man who taught the business classes and bookkeeping had a huge impact on Mildred's life work on the mission field in Liberia, West Africa. There she had three sets of books to keep: her own, the Bible school's, and the Monrovia District's financial books.

From 1948-1958, Mildred Duncklee was a teacher at Trinity Bible College in North Dakota and "mother" in the girl's dorm, while serving as District Sunday School Director for North Dakota. In 1958, she left for West Africa, where she became the principal in charge of the Newaka Girl's School with over 90 girls between the ages of 6 and 20. Her ministry in West Africa expanded as she trained Sunday school representatives and directors, started youth camps for Liberians, preached every weekend, and held seminars for pastors and church workers once a year in outlying districts. The Owensgrove Bible School was her home for 25 years as a teacher and principal.

After completing 30 years of ministry in Liberia, Africa, Mildred returned to Trinity Bible College as Missionary in Residence. In later years, Mildred resides in Hannacroix, New York, where she continues Sunday school teaching, preaching, and visitation.

Mildred's graduation from Western Pentecostal Bible College in Winnipeg, Manitoba, attendance at the University of North Dakota in Grand Forks, and life changing years at North Central made her a powerful and diverse influence in Liberia as well as the States. Her return trips to the U.S. influenced many Americans positively for missions, including the Marcus Bakke (NCBI student) family in Scranton, North Dakota. The Bakke dinner table was a place of adventure as Mildred (and many other missionaries) would answer questions and tell stories of God's grace at work in the beautiful people of Liberia. All five of the Bakke children have hearts for missions and God's work, as do the grandchildren.

Maximizing God's Provision

Henry Dahlberg, Class of 1942

The depression of the 1930's still affected students as they came to North Central to study in 1939. The wage scale was 25 cents an hour if one could get a job. One of the few available jobs was delivery of the *Minneapolis Tribune* on a paper route. I got up at 5 a.m. to deliver papers, making $12 per month. That was enough to pay room rent of $1.50 per week with a bit of change left over. Meals were a bigger problem. A standard way of getting food was by washing dishes in a café. One hour of work provided for one meal since each meal was about 25 cents. Today's meals still cost about an hour's labor. Many of the female students worked as maids for their board and room.

Chapter Two

Not only did the students struggle with survival, but the school did also. There were a few times when the administration asked for special prayer to pay for heating oil. Several times, the school was within hours of having to shut down the furnace for lack of oil. They did not have established credit and needed cash to pay for the oil. Somehow by God's help, we made it.

One tragedy was the experience of a married couple, living off campus. They ran out of food, having only onions. They told no one of their plight until they had a mental breakdown and had to leave. The school officials were so sorry; in trying to live by faith, these students did not feel free to make their needs known. In difficulty, we all learn that, as humans, it is okay to speak of our need to one another.

One of the clearest memories that stands out in my mind is the mighty move of God in early 1940 and again in 1941. Classes were not held for two or three days, as God moved and people were filled with the Holy Spirit. Some of the guys in the dorm were so desperate to be filled with God and the Holy Spirit that we met in a fourth floor room for a prayer meeting. Being a warm night, we opened the windows, while praying hard and loudly. A knock on the door was heard. There stood a Minneapolis policeman responding to complaints from the neighbors about the noise. He probably expected a noisy college party. When the policeman found out it was a prayer meeting, he politely asked us to close the windows and quietly left.

Another bit of trivia: At the corner of Chicago and 14th there was a tavern. Girls waiting for the streetcar, which stopped at Chicago and 14th, had to stand on the corner by the tavern. It was not the best of circumstances. Students prayed, and the tavern closed. The tavern/brothel became Giswold's Drug Store, known as Gissie's. That building became the NCU bookstore and the upper room a lovely classroom in about 2001. Parking lots and NCU classrooms have replaced area liquor stores.

Some students came to North Central with excellent academic

records. Others came with little or no high school education. The emphasis was on serving the Lord Jesus Christ and following in his ways. This became an important element as I became a missionary to French West Africa, which is now Burkina Faso and Togo from 1946 to 1954. At the French West African Bible School, none of the men in my classes had a formal education. They learned to read and write in their village churches! Sometimes I gave oral quizzes to fellows who could not write. I remembered back to North Central days when students were valued in spite of their formal training. It was a beautiful thing to watch as God blessed the efforts of those committed to His divine purpose.

The teachers who shared their life experiences with students made school worthwhile. A.G. Ward was a truly Pentecostal minister who was a perfect gentleman. He inspired us to live by faith. His son, C.M. Ward, was also one of our teachers, as was Ivan Miller and Frank Lindquist, all of whom we held in highest regard.

Yesterday, Today and Forever

Ida Gutel Sheneman, Class of 1943

The first chapter of my life consisted of the 19 years I spent on an Iowa farm with parents who instilled a love for God in their six children. The spiritual training I received during this time was one of the greatest blessings of my life.

The second chapter of my life lasted only four years – the years at North Central Business College that was part of North Central Bible Institute in Minneapolis, Minnesota.

The first year of Business College was fun and exciting. My father paid my tuition in the fall, but I needed money for housing and food. The school placed me in a home where I earned my room and board

Chapter Two

plus one dollar a week for streetcar fare. All I had to do was be a companion to the 12-year-old daughter in her sporting activities and baby-sit when her parents were gone. This arrangement worked quite well except for mealtime. The lady of the house did her own cooking and surprised me the first evening by putting a plate of food for me on a small table in the kitchen while their family ate in the adjoining dining room. I came from a large family where lots of conversation and companionship during meals was normal. Eating alone was not to my liking. I could not even force the food down and lost 12 pounds the first two weeks. I have said many times since, when fighting the battle of the bulge, that I should do that all over again!

I was only in Business College about two months when I was offered a position as secretary in the office of the NCBI Director of Finance. You can imagine how happy I was to accept the job and move into the dormitory. That is when I began to enjoy school in a new way and really live the good life.

The second year I was a cashier in the dining room of NCBI when a young man from Nebraska came down for breakfast with his three roommates. That first day of fall term changed my life forever. The second morning that Neale Sheneman came down to the cafeteria, his roommates were delighted to tell me that Neale talked about me in his sleep. Perhaps it was the red corduroy suit I was wearing that stuck in his memory, since red was Neale's favorite color. I do wonder what would have happened if I had been wearing blue or green. Anyway, I have thanked the Lord many times for this great blessing that came into my life – the day I wore red!

The third chapter of my life began Oct. 3, 1943, when Neale and I began our life together in Truesdale, Iowa. In the next 28 years, we pastored three churches, and traveled as evangelists for 17 years. During this time Earl Baker Sheneman was born, and grew up to marry Cindy Louise Brown. Our first grandchild, Neale Dean Sheneman II, was born to Earl and Cindy.

A Faithful Past, A Shining Future

The fourth chapter of my life involved another adventure. Numerous times throughout the years, Neale had jokingly said that someday we would live in Alaska in a log cabin in the woods. As a young girl on the cold wintry, blustery days on the Iowa farm, I would tell my mother that when I grew up, I would live in Florida. As we sought God for his will, our hearts were prepared for the challenge of starting a church in Anchorage that Neale had already named Muldoon Community Assembly, since he felt God definitely led him to that part of the city. With no financial backing nor promise of any, we knew approval of God, the Alaska district superintendent, and area ministers was what we needed.

God confirmed his calling as Neale entered the Little Beaver Lake camp meeting as the afternoon service was in progress. As he opened the camp meeting door, someone in the auditorium stood and was giving a prayer request, "Pray that God will send someone to the Muldoon area of Anchorage to start a church." The prayer request of Norma and Henry Porte was answered as God began "The Muldoon Miracle" in a rented hall in August 1971. Kent Redfearn, president of the 1983 senior class of Northwest College in Kirkland, Washington, came to work with us and became the next senior pastor of Muldoon Community Assembly.

The property on which MCA was built was three acres of woods with trails on which moose wandered back and forth. In the middle of the property was a log cabin that became our home – our rental of the log house paid for the purchase of the property.

On October 3, 1992, Neale and I celebrated our 49th wedding anniversary. On October 12th, Neale moved to Heaven, and a new chapter of my life began. Family and friends extended every kindness, and I enjoyed working in the nursery, Sunday School and loved everyone at MCA so deeply.

Bellingham, Washington is now my home as I enjoy King Mountain Assembly of God and my dear family and friends.

Chapter Two
Memoirs of a Minnesotan
Ken Freiheit, Class of 1943

One hundred and twenty-five young people enrolled as freshmen in NCBI on September 16, 1940. Our freshman days were full of new and interesting experiences since we all came from different parts of the country. However, we were soon made to feel at home by the upper classmen and the faculty. I remember the bonfire service at Powderhorn Park where we dedicated our lives to serve the Lord with all of our hearts.

Our days were very full, working part-time jobs and studying. I shall never forget our studies in the books of Job and Esther under the teaching of C.M. Ward. His insight in the scriptures was profound, and his presentation was very unique. Rev. Ward was my favorite teacher who had the most impact on my life.

I shall never forget the big Armistice Day blizzard on November 11, 1940. All classes were dismissed because the city of Minneapolis was completely paralyzed by about 60 inches of snow. My brother Merle and I invested in shovels and went to work shoveling out business places.

Four of our freshmen organized a quartet made up of Bob Abbott, George Cummings, Wesley Hurst, and Fred Lessten (all are deceased). They were known as the "Gospel Broadcasters." These fellows traveled across the country holding services, spreading the good news of Jesus' saving grace. Other students were out conducting vacation Bible schools and evangelizing.

The highlight of my junior year (1941-1942) was the experience of being filled with the Holy Spirit at the first chapel service that lasted all day. I had been seeking for this precious gift for several years. This gift gave me the confidence and power to answer God's call into the ministry. I thank the Lord for the emphasis that was given to us students to receive the Baptism of the Holy Spirit.

In the fall of 1942 during World War II, 60 of us came back for our senior year. Eleven of our classmates were serving our country in the armed forces.

It was during my senior year that I was elected president of the student council, which was challenging to say the least. I was also involved in singing in the choir and playing my cornet in the orchestra during all three years at NCBI.

After graduating in the spring of 1943, I was asked by our district superintendent to plant a church in Pipestone, Minnesota, which started with three very faithful ladies. We met in a tent for six weeks after which a nightclub building became available. After three years, we were able to build a church and parsonage. It was in 1945 that Marian Fischer and I were married, and our two boys, Douglas and Dennis, were born while in Pipestone.

Between 1950 and 1955 I was pastor of the Detroit Lakes AG where Sunday school was at the top of the list. We set a record with 260 in attendance on Easter Sunday 1955. It was during an evangelistic crusade with Joe Johnson that this record was set. A revival spirit prevailed!

In 1955 I was elected the first full-time D-CAP with the Minnesota District. This was a big challenge for me. I also taught a new course on "Youth Leadership" at the college.

In 1959 I was elected pastor of Little Falls Assembly of God. While there, we were able to plant a new church in Long Prairie. We also built a parsonage while there. In 1965 I was elected the Minnesota District Secretary/Treasurer, a position I held for 27 years. During that time, I was the editor of the Fellowship Tidings, which was the District's monthly publication. I was also the World Missions Director for the Minnesota District, and I have been the District Stewardship Director from 1982 to the present.

Chapter Two
Memoirs of a North Dakota Boy
Wells Gage, Class of 1945

Wells Gage remembered Professor Emil Balliet "because of his warm and pleasant personality. He never had any degree of partiality, which I greatly respected in view of my own background."

As a farm boy from North Dakota, Wells was a very bashful young boy. The big city and North Central were an awesome experience for him, having barely been off the Dakota farm. Classmates, staff and faculty were so kind and helpful as he made the adjustment. Wells had not been able to attend high school. He had only an elementary education before he spent time in the United States Navy. He came to NCBI after a "special order discharge." Wells reported that his interrogating officers wrote, "Wells will be of greater value to the ministry than to the US Navy." That enabled Wells to attend North Central during the war and draft years.

On March 29, 1947, Wells Gage and Yvonne Cavitch (1946 graduate) married in Washington, New Jersey, before joining Pastor Lloyd Jorgenson (1935) in Kulm, North Dakota. The Gages also served congregations in Lyons, Oregon; Conrad, Montana; and Skagway, Alaska. Though it has been over 60 years since the Gage's NCBI graduation, they continue strong in mind and focus sharing hope and love to those around them in Yuma, Arizona.

Memories of a New Yorker
Paul Sundell and Dorothy Nungesser Sundell
Class of 1950 and 1948

Paul Sundell

I shall never forget the night I arrived in Minneapolis after traveling many hours by train from New York state. I had only been restored in my walk with the Lord since June, but I knew, without question, I was called into the ministry.

My first glimpse of North Central late that evening was not the most exhilarating. I entered 910 Elliot into a poorly lit hall, and eventually was escorted to a large dorm room on the fourth floor. There were eight beds in that room. I do not recollect being in the least put off by the condition of the building. I was too excited about coming to Bible school.

The first week of school there was a chapel service every evening. What left an impression on me was the great time of seeking God. I was filled with the Holy Spirit in one evening service in an experience I will never forget.

Studying the Bible was a whole new experience for me. While I did not enjoy nor apply myself in high school, it was the opposite in Bible school. It was interesting how students soon developed a "tag" to describe each class, such as "Story Hour." My favorite classes were the ones taught by T.J. Jones. He instilled in us such an excitement and love for the Word. What really impressed me was how this man, though having preached and taught for many years, was still an ardent student of the Word.

School life was filled with activity. Most of us, as students, had part time jobs. So after the last class we were off to work. One year I worked at the school operating the elevator. That was fun, because I really had opportunities to develop friendships with many of the students. One in particular was Dorothy Nungesser, class of 1948. She worked as one of the secretaries in the office, and so we had opportunities to see each other quite often. The outcome of that is now history, over 55 years together.

There was usually something interesting going on around 910 Elliot. One escapade I recall was of dropping water-filled balloons from the roof on those entering the building. Because of some

Chapter Two

former experience working in a meat market, Ida Jensma had me cutting up some of the beef that came for the cafeteria (umm – nice steaks!)

Dorothy was in the senior class that graduated in 1948. After school, she worked at Sears and in 1949 we were married at the Minneapolis Gospel Tabernacle. Working our way through school wasn't that impossible when the tuition was $75 a semester. Dorothy was the class secretary and enjoyed choir. I also enjoyed singing in choir and playing in the school orchestra with my bass horn.

Graduation time came for me in May 1950. Two other students and I made a trip to Indiana prior to graduation to attend the District Council. While there, I applied for a license with the Indiana District. After graduation, I was off to Indiana in hopes of finding a place for ministry. Within one week, and through a series of steps that were God-directed, I was asked to pastor a brand new home mission work in Lowell, a small town in northwest Indiana of about 2,000. Though they could offer no salary, I was so excited to become their first pastor! I immediately returned to Minneapolis to get Dorothy and our few belongings and return to Lowell. Those were great days of learning what it was to "live by faith."

After pastoring the Assembly of God in Brazil, Indiana, we pastored churches in Barnesville and Faribault, Minnesota.

From there we went as missionaries to Belgium, to work in the French speaking Immanuel Bible Institute in Andrimont, France, which was close to the German border. Both Dorothy and I learned the French language, using our new language to teach at IBI for three years.

People from many countries and languages were expressing need for more Biblical knowledge. God laid dreams and need on the hearts of ordinary men and women to expand IBI to a school with broader cultural, geographical/linguistic base. We worked with Charles Greenway and others in setting the vision; recruitment and raising of funding; property acquisition; curriculum development; care of legal matters; staff, faculty, and student recruitment details; and thus realized the establishment of Continental Bible College in centrally located Brussels, Belgium. Training at NCBI laid the framework upon which the dream of a new school could be spawned.

The influence of T.J. Jones laid the ground work for my passion to understand the Word of God. T.J. Jones lived the Bible – he lived in the Bible. This powerful impact motivated me in everything I did.

After spending six years in Brussels, we moved back to Minneapolis, where we taught for two years at NCBC. The next decade we pastored the great Minneapolis Gospel Tabernacle, now known as Christ Church International. It was during that time that MGT opened its new sanctuary (late 1970's) and continued to expand its effectiveness in the Twin Cities.

St. Clair Shores, Michigan, became our next home for almost two decades. There we pastored and served as Dean of the CBC Extension School in Detroit.

Since retirement, we have moved back to Minneapolis where we are active at Christ Church International, and also have traveled to several European countries, teaching in our Bible colleges in Portugal, Lithuania, Moscow, Mexico City, and Capetown, South Africa.

It is thrilling to see how North Central University has grown and developed, but is still proclaiming the Pentecostal message.

Continental Bible College is now known as Continental Theological Seminary. It continues as a strong, healthy, growing educational institution. Its leadership and foundation, laid by godly NCU men and women, follows the biblical model of II Timothy 2:2. ("Train others so that they may train others also") that the world might know Him.

Chapter Two
World War II Veterans Come To NCBC

Milton John Kersten and Dorothy Wilke Kersten
Class of 1949

Many NCBI students' studies were interrupted by WWII. Some returned and some were unable. Jonathan Liechty attended NCBI one year before being drafted into the United States Army. Though he was unable to return, his daughter, Sherri Liechty Owen attended NCBC in the 1970's. Sherri and her husband, Bill Owen, have gone on to teach and head up the music department at Northwest College in Kirkland, Washington. Jonathan Liechty's influence grew throughout the years as he returned years later to serve on the Board of Regents for NCBC.

The end of World War II, 1945, brought dynamic changes to the student body of NCBC.

Vets were different than prior enrollees: the average age was higher; many were already married; military training and war experience had matured them beyond their years; and they seemed more settled and serious about pursuing what they believed to be God's purpose for their lives. Veterans felt welcome at NCBI.

Typical of the veteran enrollees is one student who started in 1946. I was drafted into the army at the age of 18. I spent one year in technical training and two years in the South Pacific, serving in a medical unit that cared for the sick and wounded. When the U.S. Army liberated the Philippines, my unit received the American prisoners of war from their years of internment in Bildad Prison, Manila.

Suddenly, with the atomic bombing of Nagasaki and Hiroshima the war ended. Within months I was home in Wausau, Wisconsin, and the big question was, "Now what?" My mother welcomed me with, "I said good bye to my little boy. Now I see you as a mature man. What are your plans?" God had already made His call clear, gospel ministry and foreign missions. An interesting episode contributed to that sense of call.

Before sailing to the island of New Guinea, a Christian buddy and I were able to get weekend passes to San Francisco, California. We decided to find Glad Tidings Bible Institute and visited two classes. One of the teachers was T.J. Jones. After the class the future NCBI student said, "Would I ever like to sit under that man's teaching!" In 1946 I enrolled in NCBI to discover that 1946 was the year that the venerable and greatly loved T.J. Jones began his teaching ministry there.

This typical vet graduated from NCBI in 1949 with a vision and a sense of Bible know-how to plant two churches in the U.S. (Oneida and Seymour, Wisconsin) and then give over 35 years as an appointed Assemblies of God missionary in church growth and advanced Christian education.

Friendships forged at NCBI have endured the decades. Only God knows the impact of the lives that sat together under the same chalk dust and then fanned out around planet earth in obedience to our Savior and Commander, Jesus Christ.

A brief biographical history follows:

Stillwater, Minnesota in 1948: North Central Bible Institute students called the Quintet (Calvin Olson, Milton Kersten, Ben Mazurek, Merwin Price, and Gerald Fisher) started meetings in Stillwater, Minnesota at the Odd Fellows Hall. Marlin Peterson joined them later. After some years this developed into the Stillwater Assemblies of God Church.

Cornell, Wisconsin in 1947: Dorothy Wilke (later Kersten) went with Clara Wilcox (Krake) to plant a church in the small city of Cornell. The church building was built in 1949-1950. Dorothy left later in 1949 when she was called home to take care of sickness in her parent's home, and she married Milton Kersten in 1950.

Chapter Two

Seymour, Wisconsin in 1951-1961: December, 1951 Milton and Dorothy (Wilke) Kersten moved to Seymour to establish a church. With the congregation, they first remodeled a house for parsonage and then built a fine church building.

Oneida, Wisconsin in 1952-1958: At the same time that Kerstens started meetings in Seymour, they were invited by the Oneida Indian folk to start house meetings. That developed into a fine congregation who worked with Milton in building a lovely church edifice. Sons Daniel and Phil were born during these years and benefited from the nurturing strength of Oneida and Seymour friends.

Guyana (formerly British Guiana), South America 1962-1976: Milton and Dorothy Kersten went as foreign missionaries. They worked there 14 years in establishing churches, training ministers, helping in national offices until the work was indigenous throughout.

1976-1989: Milton Kersten worked seventeen years as Area Representative for eight countries in the Caribbean. He also started the Caribbean School of Theology in 1982, conducting seminars in that area in advanced studies for national ministers. Kersten then served from 1990-1993 as Special Assistant to Field Director John Bueno.

1993-present: Though retired, the Kerstens fill in at area churches as needed for short or longer term responsibilities as God provides strength.

Seek First the Kingdom of God

Marcus Bakke
NCBI student from 1948-1949

I was born and raised in southwestern North Dakota on a farm near the city of New England. In 1946, an Assemblies of God group came to our town and began holding meetings. In the summer prior to my conversion, a singing trio of NCBI students, Roger, Betty Jane and Mary Ellen Haas, visited our new assembly and told us about a wonderful Bible college in Minneapolis, Minnesota. My sister, Alice May Bakke, enrolled that fall of 1947.

In January 1948, at the age of 20, I became a "born again" Christian. Three months later, I received the Baptism of the Holy Spirit. It was during that experience I offered myself to God for ministry. It was a defining moment in my life. Following my conversion, I made a trip to Minneapolis and visited the college. That fall I enrolled and became one of 150-plus freshmen. It was quite an adventure for a timid, newly saved farm boy.

Here are some of the things I remember about North Central that had an influence in shaping the early months of my spiritual development.

I remember the impact of the wonderful chapel services. The spirited singing, anointed preaching, and operation of the gifts of the Holy Spirit were very inspiring for me. It gave me a good understanding of our Pentecostal message and heritage.

I remember being in classes taught by godly teachers such as T. J. Jones, Brother Edson, Ione Soltau, Maxine Williams, D.V. Hurst and others. I do not recall much of what they said, but I do remember HOW they said it. It seemed to me, though, that mercy was not always a consideration for some students who were not academically inclined. One of my roommates felt like the tribulation was happening. I spent a lot of time helping him survive his English class. Wow! Precious memories. I was fortunate – I CLEPed English!

I remember the meaningful times of prayer. I had a favorite place that I would frequent to get alone and talk to God about His call on my life. It was in the basement furnace area of Miller Hall where the student traffic was light. These were important times of spiritual growth for me.

I remember the blessing and thrill of traveling on weekends to

Chapter Two

various churches for ministry. I recall going to Pillager, Minnesota with the Rev. G. Raymond Carlson and his wife for a special service. I was one of the fortunate students who came to school with an automobile. It did help with the popularity issue, especially if you were willing to take a load of students with you.

I remember the Washington Street Gospel Mission Ministry in which some of us were involved. These were important ministry opportunities where we could view the effect the world had on men who lost their direction in life. We found this was a good place to get practical and valuable ministry experience that would become useful later in ministry when working with alcoholics and people of the street. It was a great experience.

I remember learning that it is not all gold that glitters. I was a naive young farm boy who thought that all who went to Bible school were focused and had serious spiritual ambitions in life. I was soon to learn differently. I learned it was wise to choose friends who were going somewhere with God and who were willing to leave their worldly ways and pursuits behind. I learned things about people that helped me in my spiritual understanding and development.

I remember the opportunities I had to become acquainted with some of the older students, many who had served in the military. They were, for the most part, no-nonsense guys who were great examples of commitment and dedication to the call of God. I doubt if they realized what a positive influence they were to many of us younger students. They became our mentors. I cherish those memories and relationships.

I remember the great roommates I had. All were sincere students who desired God's will for their lives. We shared serious and not-so-serious moments. We became good friends. One of them was a good guitar player so we sang and had good times. Another was quite a profound sermonizer, so we listened! We made lasting friendships that have survived through the years.

A Faithful Past, A Shining Future

I remember the major sport with guys on our floor was ping-pong. Wow! Some of those guys were good. I am glad to see that NCU now has a gymnasium!

In the spring of 1949, I left NCBI and did not have the privilege of continuing my Bible college education. I married a beautiful young lady, Elva Mae Bjorum from Hettinger, North Dakota. We found ourselves involved in a very small church in Scranton, a small town of 314 people on the prairie of southwestern North Dakota. In 1950, we committed ourselves to ministry there, which developed and continued in that city for the next 25 years. We began a radio broadcast in 1955 that lasted for the next 25 years.

While pastoring at Scranton, we also pastored a small church in Rhame. When that work became self-sustaining, we turned it over to a fine worker. We then began an outreach in Bowman where a wonderful church was established which we pastored for five years prior to becoming the district superintendent of the North Dakota District of the Assemblies of God. I served as a sectional presbyter for nine years, assistant superintendent for 13 years, and district superintendent for 19 years.

Following our retirement from the district office in 1999, we committed ourselves to a non-profit challenge on the Standing Rock Indian Reservation at Selfridge, North Dakota. The small church was no longer functioning. We accepted the challenge, opened the church, and are now ministering regularly on the reservation. We have seen a number of lives influenced by the gospel and look forward to each time we go to minister to the people in that area.

I feel that my experience at North Central Bible Institute was a major influence for good in my development as a young minister. I am thankful for those who have given and sacrificed to build and maintain our Bible colleges. I am grateful for the dedicated teachers and workers who inspired and challenged my faith and inspired trust in us for God and man. My year at North Central was a positive influence in my life. It was vital to my understanding and philosophy of Christian life and ministry. I have no regrets for the year I spent at North Central.

Gentleman Scholar

Donald and Norma Huisinga Tanner, Class of 1953 and 1951

North Central Bible College provided for those of us who were undergrads in the 1950's a high-quality education that prepared us for our life's work. My wife, Norma (Huisinga, 1951) and I (1953) are humble recipients of the dedication of the faculty and students at North Central and the Pentecostal heritage we received. North Central was, and still is, totally committed to excellence through the role models of faculty and staff.

Our undergraduate years were filled with fellow students who have remained our close friends to the present. The North Central faculty was unsurpassed in the knowledge and skills presented on a daily basis. NCBI provided an environment that enabled Norma and me to fulfill the various facets of our ministry. At that time, possibly some of us did not even know what direction our lives and ministry would take, but the faculty consistently prepared us for what came. For us, whether it was as an associate pastor at Calvary Temple in Winnipeg, full-time evangelists for over 10 years, a faculty member at NCU for 12 years, or careers in a public university for over 25 years, our early education enabled us to find the answers that applied to each situation. One of the highlights of our undergraduate years was the Pentecostal emphasis that prevailed on campus. Norma and I are proud to be Pentecostal with our roots deeply anchored in our North Central background.

In 1965 the North Central Bible College faculty became my

colleagues as I accepted a teaching position that had a 12-year tenure. At first, I taught classes for Dr. John Phillipps who was on a sabbatical leave. The help that Dr. Phillipps gave me in preparing to teach his classes was invaluable, and without it, I would have faltered badly. He was an outstanding example of North Central's fine professors. When he returned, I assumed other classes including English Composition, Romans, and classes in music.

Following the excellent ministry and musical leadership of the Rev. L.B. Larsen, I directed and toured with the Evangelaires, and toured as the speaker with the Gospel Hymns directed by the Rev. Oral Krans. Never have we forgotten the deep impressions made by Frank Lindquist, I.O. Miller, T.J. Jones, John Phillipps, Ray Levang, Marvin Nelson, Esther Selness, and the many others who left indelible impressions upon our lives. In fact, 50 years later we still have class notes from Brothers Lindquist, Miller, and Jones. Our North Central years on the faculty, 1965-1977, were wonderful years for us as a family. The faculty that I had admired so greatly became our family, and the student body became a strong encouragement and incentive in our ministry. In some small way, I wanted to have a ministry at North Central in which I could emulate, (or repay if you please) those who had so admirably shaped our lives. The Pentecostal heritage that was born years earlier at NCU was just as prevalent in our lives at that time as it had been when we were students.

The North Central experiences (1965-1977) also adequately prepared me for a career in a large public university. As a professor and chair of music education at Texas Tech University (1977-2001), I had the opportunity to help shape the ideas and thinking of university students who were seeking purpose in their lives. Sermonizing from our evangelistic days (1953-1957 and 1959-1965) was not only a wonderful ministry, but also was good preparation for my university career as it gave me confidence in expressing my ideas and beliefs before people. Norma will soon complete 30 years at the

Chapter Two

university's School of Law. We were both well-served by North Central.

North Central University nurtured an academic environment that stimulated learning – not only academic learning but learning through the examples of the faculty and staff. Outpourings of the Holy Spirit are still vivid. The chapel of 910 Elliot Avenue holds wonderful memories of dynamic speakers, sermons that shaped our lives, and Pentecostal experiences that validated what we studied in class.

In looking back, Norma and I would not change one thing. We are what we are because of the goodness of God, and because of the excellent education we received both academically and spiritually. We have enjoyed a wonderful life, crowned with spiritual blessings and good health, and have also had the privilege of doing what we enjoyed most: ministry. Our prayer is that God's blessings will continue to rest upon North Central University, the Board of Regents, the President, the administrators, faculty, staff, and students.

Faculty, administrative or staff persons who most impacted my life are listed below.

Dr. John Phillipps was a first-rate professor. I enjoyed studying Greek with him as well as many other courses. It was my privilege to substitute for him when he was on Sabbatical, and his help to me at that time was more than anyone could wish for. Dr. and Mrs. Phillipps have been wonderful friends.

Dr. Frank Lindquist was an extraordinary teacher, president and person. We greatly enjoyed our evangelistic ministry at the Minneapolis Gospel Tabernacle when he pastored there.

Not only was the I.O. Miller's administrative skill invaluable, but his knowledge in the classroom is memorable.

T.J. Jones' teaching and preaching were stimulating and insightful. He never lacked for material that had great purpose.

Marvin Nelson made a great contribution to North Central as the Dean of Education. He made everything work smoothly.

Esther Selness was the head of the Music department during our undergraduate days. She was unselfish in her concern for students' success and a very inspiring individual, indeed.

L.B. Larsen was an excellent professor and a superb choir director. His choral groups excelled. He and his wife, Wilma, were wonderful people with a great heart for ministry.

Dr. Donald Argue became the Dean of Education during my teaching tenure. He was the finest man with whom to work and brought a strong sense of academic purpose to the college at that time. He is a masterful educator.

Many other faculty and staff members established themselves as close friends and colleagues. They all had a very special place in the history of North Central University.

Open Doors – My Story

The Rev. D.V. Hurst, Class of 1951

Ministry? No!! Yes!!

Not only did I never plan to go into education as a vocation, I never really planned to go into the ministry, either. When Dad was voted out of a church once, Wes and I were in the furnace room of the church, crying. I swore that I would "never go into the ministry." I remember, however, as a small boy I played between the church and parsonage in Annandale and I suddenly became aware that I would be in ministry.

While walking home from church one Sunday night in the late spring of my senior year, one of my friends asked, "Well, Dewey, what are you going to do?" I casually replied, " I'm going to North Central and going into the ministry." "What?" she said. "You are?!" And I reaffirmed it. When we got home, she spilled it out to Mom and Dad and that was it. Surprise reigned! And of course, Mother was glad and Dad was pleased. I followed through on that since it was a deep commitment riding under the facade I had carried.

To North Central Bible Institute as Student

During the summer before school started, I went to Minneapolis to work at a job that my brother Wes had told me about. I lived in the dorm and my roommate was Lester Borner, a business college student. We played pranks on the night watchman. At the 50th anniversary of North Central when such things were being discussed, a good friend said, "Have you ever repented of that?"

As I continued at North Central through my first year, I joined a quartet—each class had one—and traveled with Peter Brooks, Bayard Carlson and Sherrill Paulson during the summer of 1942. The war was on, and we used Bayard's car. The tires were worn, and gas was scarce. We drove 45 miles per hour as required during the war. We managed gas rationing by getting extra coupons from some parishioners.

One of the services we held was in Thief River Falls where G. Raymond Carlson was pastor. I played my baritone horn and sang baritone in the quartet, and Bayard played his mandolin. Peter had a deep base voice and could sing even lower than a Russian Basso Profundo, who we read about in *Reader's Digest*.

The second time I met Aggie was in Sioux Falls, South Dakota. After the church service Aggie and I sat in the living room talking until late. She was a fantastic conversationalist, to say the least, and she was witty and cute, too. The next day, I had her application for North Central in hand along with the $10 application fee to take back to North Central. Her mother was especially pleased that Aggie was thinking of going to North Central and encouraged her.

When she arrived at NCBI, I made sure Aggie's once-in-every-two-week dates were "tied-up." (Freshmen were allowed to date only once every two weeks. For nine months that meant a maximum of

18.) On our first 'date' we went across Chicago Avenue to the Band Box for hamburgers – five cents each! Well, I forgot my billfold in the room and Aggie had to pay! So much for the first date.

When I returned to school, I got a job along with Wes and a couple other students, working for a "private detective." We rode the streetcars and buses "spying" on the operators and reporting each day. We received specific assignments to ride certain buses and streetcars. We also could freelance as much as we chose. We were paid 71 cents per hour – good pay and long hours.

Aggie

Most of my dates with Aggie were going to church together. There was nothing heavily romantic about that. We talked and gradually understood that we would get married after I graduated. This, too, was the pattern followed by most of the students. We talked some about her background as an MK in Africa, but at no time did I sense "pause" because of it. I was interested in her as she was. I don't recall exactly when I read the book *Jungle Trails* that her mother had written. It was the first hardbound volume published by the Gospel Publishing House in Springfield, Missouri.

In our conversations I did learn of her illness including the heavy infection she had while in high school, an infection so severe she missed one year. It was an infection in her face and her upper lip swelled and hung down over her lower lip. They feared for her life because the doctors were not able to "whip" it. Of course they didn't have the antibiotics that are available today. I also learned of her malaria, fevers, and intestinal infections, all a holdover from Africa. It wasn't until her final illness that the rickets showed up, and her one leg became very weak and her ankle turned, as she describes the problem in her book.

Roommates my junior year were my brother Wes, Bob Abbott and Ken Freiheit. After Ken graduated in 1943, we conducted two revival meetings together that summer between my junior and senior years. Ken and I alternated preaching in a storefront church pioneered by Norman Bratvold in Bovey, Minnesota. We slept in a room in the back of the store and spent the remainder of the summer in Aberdeen, South Dakota, singing on the radio. Later in life, I worked with the Assemblies of God radio program Revivaltime known for reaching "across the nation and around the world."

John Phillipps and Parliamentary Procedures

John Phillipps became class president and I became vice president for both of our junior and senior years. John was older and fairly well versed in doctrine. So, we studied together many nights, reviewing the study questions and answers as they were given to us. As I look back, I'm aware that the study experience with him was a major turning point for me as well as him. John went on to seminary and then taught at North Central for decades. A new residence hall is named for him.

During my senior year I took the parliamentary law course, as all seniors did. F.J. Lindquist taught the course and used the technique of having the class organize a church from scratch. In between sessions of organization he discussed the chapters in the book emphasizing basic principles. This, of course, was a good teaching technique, since he could interrupt as we went along and comment on what we did right and what we did wrong. I quickly learned that at the close of every class we should formally recess and/or adjourn. To recess would be appropriate since we were to continue in the next class session.

One time the class dispersed quickly without any formal action. I got three or four fellows together that night, and we went back into the room. We continued the session, appointing an acting chairman and an acting secretary. Then we proceeded to take action. We quickly voted all the ladies out of the church. Thus they could not vote. Then we changed the name of the church and did other things. On purpose we did not call attention to the fact that we had no quorum.

When the class meeting convened the next time and the minutes were read, the traditional question was asked: "Any corrections or additions?" Our secretaries then stood to say, "Yes, there are some additions." He then read the minutes of our "rump" meeting and moved they be added. One of us seconded the motion, and then the motion was before the class. The class sat stunned, and F.J. Lindquist wondered what to do. The men of the class quickly saw the fun involved and stood with us. Some, however, tried to declare the meeting was illegal because we had no quorum. We made it clear that no one had challenged that in the "rump" meeting, as it really was a continuation of the previous meeting. Of course we made it clear, too, that the previous meeting had not been legally closed.

The girls tried to be involved, and we said they could not since they had been put out of the church. The "battle" continued through the whole period without resolution. Finally F.J. declared the whole action "null and void" and led in recessing the meeting. Class was then dismissed. In the whole process, however, many parliamentary principles were reviewed and underscored. No discipline or retribution of any kind followed our action.

My Holy Spirit Baptism

Here I was, graduated after three years in North Central. I had traveled in ministry with a quartet for a summer. I had engaged in evangelistic meetings and then sung on a gospel radio broadcast. But, although I was in a Pentecostal movement and heading for a ministry in it, I had not been baptized in the Holy Spirit!

Although I had sought the experience and had prayed in the Lake Geneva Camp prayer room along with hundreds of others who did experience their baptism, I still had not. Shortly after I graduated, an evangelist, Anna B. Lock, a converted prostitute, was holding a meeting in Fremont Tabernacle in north Minneapolis. She strummed her guitar and sang and preached. She had a ministry in "getting people through to the baptism" and knew my folks. The first night I was there she met me in the aisle at the close of the service and poked her finger in my chest and asked, "Dewey, how do you expect to preach it if you haven't got it?" That set me to thinking seriously.

I attended the meeting again the next night, and at the close of the service I went to the prayer room and began seeking in earnest... almost desperation. Soon I raised my hands and almost immediately began to speak in tongues. Quickly I pulled my hands down and stopped, thinking, "This is not it. This is too easy. This is the 'flesh.'"

Just at that moment Anna Lock came by and, sensing what was taking place, said, "Dewey, that's God. You let go and let God!" So, I did and the Spirit moved and the tongues language rolled. When I finished, the pastor, Russell Olson, who later became a great friend, said, "That's just what you needed. You needed to have the starch taken out of you." Then I knew I was on my way to being ready to "preach it."

To North Central As Faculty

Aggie and I were at the Wisconsin camp meeting for a few days. Dad was still pastoring in Superior, Wisconsin, and was involved in district work. At this time a phone call came from NCBI saying that Mark Bell, English faculty at NCBI, had resigned. He and I had struck up a friendly relationship my senior year while I was editor of the *Archive* and he was the *Archive* advisor. I became the prospect in Emil Balliet's mind to fulfill this position.

We went to NCBI where I was interviewed for the job by F.J. Lindquist, Ivan Miller and Emil Balliet. Later into the interview F.J. asked me how old I was. I said, "I'll be 24 in October." In September there I was with Aggie, and I was teaching 17 hours and serving as Practical Work Director because several other people had gone elsewhere, and I was the only replacement.

I was assigned to teach English Composition to the freshman

class of 135 students. I had a good textbook and assigned a theme – "Why I came to North Central." You guessed it! I had to read and mark 135 themes, along with all the other preparation for the 17 hours I was teaching. I remember sitting in our living room night after night and reading those themes. I quickly decided that couldn't go on. But I learned what the students needed as I read those papers.

For my third year I also was asked to direct the choir by pastor Russell Olson at Old Fremont Tabernacle. This was a break. I've often said, "I went into debt the first year teaching – couldn't pay the rent to the school – broke even the second year and paid my debts the third year and then left." The $25 from Fremont Tabernacle that I received twice a month was just enough to give to Aggie to buy groceries. So we were able to pay our debts.

As a freshman faculty in 1947, I served as advisor for the *Archive*. Each year someone was given special honor in the yearbook. Manuel Schoults, editor, spearheaded the effort to honor Treasurer Herb Snyder, who had never been honored in the yearbook, though he had served many years at North Central. Manuel Schoults later served as district superintendent in Northern Missouri district for many years.

It was an honor to be invited back as a special guest for the 50th reunion of the class of 1950. It was also an honor to be invited back as a special guest for the 50th anniversary of North Central along with Morris Williams and G. Raymond Carlson.

Guided My Vision

Dorothy Olson Cederblom, Class of 1952

Larry and Dorothy Cederblom were missionaries in Latin America (Dominican Republic and Panama) from 1961-2005. They established the Resource and Advisory Center for Bible Schools of Latin America in 1995, while doing extensive traveling and teaching professors in the Bible schools.

My memories of NCBI include the Rev. T.J. Jones, who was approachable and easy to talk with. His teaching was heart-felt and deep, causing much spiritual challenge, which fill my thoughts to this day. In 1955, he was the officiating minister at our wedding.

John Phillipps was a great teacher and friend. He was brilliant and knowledgeable in many areas. His consistent Christian life and ethics were an example to all of us.

North Central strongly impacted my life and guided my vision and dedication for missionary work these last 44 years.

I Am a Debtor

Ernest J. and Gladys Dewahl Moen, Class of 1953

Yes, I am a debtor to North Central University. It has been my good fortune to have an invaluable and priceless lifelong relationship with the college. May I enumerate my reasons?

First, the student life experiences. Relationships were made that last to this day. Norman Tosten was my roommate. We were in each other's weddings and both served the Illinois and Iowa districts as district superintendent at the same time.

It was at North Central that I met my life's companion. Nothing can compare to the mystery of ongoing love of more than 52 years, both in marriage and ministry. It could not have happened without NCU. I am a debtor.

Secondly, the fulfillment of life's call. It was at NCU where I realized God's call on my life was real. I have had many opportunities of ministry in the chapel pulpit. Nothing thrills my heart more than the inter-generational response to fulfill the great commission's mandate. For 22 years, I had the privilege of serving on the Board of Regents, serving as Chairman of the Board for 12 of those years. In those years, I observed numerical growth from 400 to nearly 1,200 students.

The greatest blessing was the bestowal of an Honorary Doctorate and the establishment of the Ernest J. Moen Chair of Pentecostal Preaching. My prayer is that scores of young people will take the gospel to the ends of the earth before the "parousia."

Thirdly, the anointed faculty to which I am most grateful – who sharpened my sword.

Marvin Nelson taught me sermon construct. Frank Lindquist was the embodiment of doctrinal certitude. I admired his skill as a Bible teacher, his unswerving convictions, and administrative skills. Ivan Miller was the epitome of holiness personified. G. Raymond Carlson cast the standard of pastoral life. He was a man of care and compassion, illustrating the practical nature of the gospel. John Phillipps taught me to love scriptural exposition. He was incredibly intelligent and the best Bible expositor ever!

Fourthly, life-long friendships. Frank Lindquist's biographer, Hart Armstrong, included words in his Lindquist biography, which I accidentally found. They were written by Irene Lindquist and addressed to my wife and me:

> Dear Ernest and Gladys,
> You have been such a blessing to Frank and myself. We are so proud to have you as a graduate of NCBC. You are a great man of God. Hope this book is a blessing to you,
> In His Love,
> Irene

To think that a busy college president's wife would take time to write words of encouragement to a graduate illustrates the quality of people at NCBC, while providing a model from which we can all benefit.

I admit – I am a debtor.

(Romans 1: 14)

A View From the Kitchen – Our Favorite Place!
Betty Hintz, Class of 1954

From 1951-1972, I worked in and managed the cafeteria for North Central. During the summers when the cafeteria was closed, I did child evangelism and conducted vacation Bible schools throughout Wisconsin, Minnesota, South Dakota, and Montana. I did chalk artistry with two singing groups, The Joyfulaires and Notes of Gladness.

Faculty who had the most impact on my life include Ione Soltau and Estelle Burkhart. Many nights, Ione and Estelle would meet with some of us in the Chapel to seek God. They prayed with students who wanted to be filled with the Holy Spirit.

I appreciated Ione Soltau's vibrant work, life and love for the Lord, and her exceptional ministry to children and the elderly. She had a big heart for giving to those in need – and to those who were not so needy. She was amazing at chalking colored pictures while presenting the gospel message. Her work inspired me to do 'chalking' in children's ministry.

During my senior year, Evelyn Hultquist King and I served as co-directors of the Women's department under Ione Soltau. Through this experience, I learned how to serve others.

Partners for Progress Banquets

Since I was in the food business, I have some unique "food related" memories of NCU. The first Partners for Progress Banquet was served at North Central with the dining room bulging with 110 people. A good "kick-off" chicken special was on the menu. Year two, Swiss steak was served and transported to Covenant Church where the banquet was held. More friends than anticipated attended, so a number of the steaks had to be cut in half.

Picnics

The all-school fall and spring picnics were highlights at North Central for many years and still are. We would pack food and meet at Como Park in St. Paul. After eating lots of food and chocolate milk, everyone would gather around the large fire, sing songs and worship God. Usually, one of the teachers would bring a message from the Bible.

Revivals

One morning in 1955, Celeste Stelter was filled with the Holy Spirit during chapel. She spoke in the heavenly language for hours. The Spirit of God moved on everyone in the building. No one went to the cafeteria to eat, classes were delayed, and the fasting, praise and prayers continued for three weeks.

During another chapel service, Laura Evans, giving her all to the Lord, took out her billfold and laid it on the altar. As the spirit of the Lord spread through the student body, confessions and rededications were made. It was a life-changing time.

Do as Much...For as Many...For as Long...

E. Louise Miller Crawford (Robert P. Crawford)
Class of 1954

The faculty member who most impacted my life was Arvid Kingsriter, my teacher, choir director and pastor. While attending

Chapter Two

NCBI, I was a member of the Evangelaires Choir, directed by Arvid Kingsriter. We traveled to various churches and performed for special occasions at school. Being in Evangelaires was a fantastic experience. I was enjoyed involvement in a traveling trio with Joanne Montag, Chris Sellers and Lou Miller and ladies chorus with Director Bud Larsen.

During our time at the school, founders I.O. Miller and Frank Lindquist prayed and felt impressed that a church was needed in the south suburban area. Arvid Kingsriter, then a teacher and Evangelaire director, became the new pastor of the Bloomington Assembly of God Church located in the "Old Kimball School House" located on the corner of 86th and Cedar in Bloomington. The first service was held in March 1954, and the Evangelaires sang at that first service.

Eventually, a new church building was built at 94th and Portland in Bloomington, and eventually moved to 8600 Bloomington Ave. South, which is the current location. In 2003, it became known as Cedar Valley Church. Our beloved pastor, Arvid Kingsriter, remained the pastor of Bloomington Assembly where we attended for nearly 50 years. Therefore and without a doubt, he provided the most long-term impact on our lives. He dedicated and performed the marriages of both our daughters Cheryl and Cindy to Steve and Bob and dedicated our grandchildren. He was a wonderful shepherd, leader and example to our entire family.

While at Bloomington Assembly of God, my husband and I were blessed to serve in many capacities including women's ministries president and vice president, choir member and primary Sunday school teacher for 18 years. We also served on the mission board and helped to establish the very first mission trips. Trips one and two were to Costa Rica with the Ken Dahlagers. The emphasis on missions that took root in our hearts at North Central University continued to grow, as more international ministry opportunities became possible including trips to Panama, Peru, Argentina, and Bolivia. Hosting missionaries in our home was a delight and our own mission field was realized as Robert and I served as foster parents to nine foster children.

A good thought that motivated my life was: "Do as much as you can – for as many as you can – for as long as you can."

North Central University provided direction and valuable knowledge for life. The years of school provided Christian affirmation, exercise in faith building, confidence in God, and long-term friendships. Looking back, these were some of the happiest years of my life.

I am thrilled with all the positive advancements made by 'our' school and I commend the past and present leaders.

Discipline and Devotion

John and Joanne Ohlin
Interview by Dr. Carolyn Tennant, Feb. 2005

When John and Joanne Ohlin were students at North Central Bible Institute from 1951 to 54, the school only offered a three-year curriculum. Shortly after this, it was expanded to four. Nonetheless, it was enough time for these two to find each other.

Joanne worked in the library and also delivered mail around the campus. Majoring in Christian Education, she was also involved in musical groups including the choir and the Evangelaires. The directors of the Evangelaires were L.B. Larsen and Arvid Kingsriter. T.J. Jones often went out with the Evangelaires on tour and preached.

"T.J. Jones loved books," said Joanne, "and he always related well to students." Jones apparently was aware that John had been noticing Joanne and spending an unusual amount of time in the library. One

Chapter Two

day while Joanne was working on arranging Jones' own books, he hinted, "Well, there's John. Have you been up in the library today?"

Jones was British and invited the students for tea at his home in Prior Lake. "It was very proper," said Joanne, "and we were a little nervous about it. We didn't really know how to act." The Ohlins also enjoyed faculty members John Phillipps, Amos Levang, and Arvid Kingsriter who shared many personal stories.

Uniforms had just ended at the North Central at this time, but the women could not wear slacks or even sweaters without a blouse under it. The students also went ice skating in the park. "My roommate and I both played saxophone," recalled Joanne, "and so sometimes we would open our window and play the "Skater's Waltz." They also remembered great class picnics. "It was a highlight of our lives in every way," said Joanne. "It was fun but also spiritual, and I grew up a ton." The Ohlins said there were various two-day revivals where there were confessions and Spiritual Emphasis with night chapels.

Since Joanne was from the Twin Cities area students often came out to her church on Sunday and ended up at her house. "My mother would put on a whole pot of soups or beans and feed them all," she said.

"Our many friendships have continued," stated John. He remembers preaching in a church with the Evangelaires. They were singing right before his message and selected the song, "Just a Closer Walk With Thee." However, the girls somehow got the giggles with a part they did ("walk a little, talk a little") and left him to preach afterwards. He remembers not being overly happy with these difficult circumstances. On top of everything, it was the first time Joanne was to hear him preach.

The Ohlins left NCBC and had a powerful life of ministry. They pastored in John's home town of Oshkosh. He became the D-Cap (District Youth Director) in Wisconsin, and Joanne was the Missionettes director. Later, John served as the director of the MAPS program and then was in Home Missions. He took early retirement in 1997 but is still involved in Health Care Ministries. Joanne served as the women's ministries leadership training coordinator until 1995.

As if this weren't enough, John has coordinated all of the General Councils for the last 20 years. Consider the administrative skills necessary for such a daunting task!

"North Central's classes helped prepare me for the ministry," said John. "I learned discipline and devotion."

The Best Days

Arvid Kingsriter and Marian Menzie Kingsriter
Class of 1941 and 1945

My years at North Central were filled with good memories. I sensed a call to the ministry when I was twelve years old. I always looked forward to preparing myself for ministry at North Central. When my high school football coach spoke to me about playing football in college, I never gave it any consideration. *My* plans were to attend North Central.

Highlights of my NCU experience include my biblical classes, an integral part of my training. Who can forget Rev. T. J. Jones in the classroom? He was filled with biblical knowledge and wanted us to have the same kind of knowledge. He did not make it easy for his students. We were given 50 chapter titles for the book of Genesis. It was our responsibility to memorize those titles before the exam. Yes, Brother Jones had high expectations of his students.

Memories also include working on the school yearbook, the *Archive*. Students would be in classes in the morning, go to work in the afternoon, work on the *Archive* at night, and get up early in the morning to study. It was a busy time, but it was a good time.

Chapter Two

Intramural basketball filled our Tuesday evenings, and I also played on a school basketball team that played other schools on Saturday nights. In addition to their excellent classroom skills, Dr. John Phillipps and Dr. Raymond Levang were our coaches.

The highlight of my North Central experience was the emphasis North Central gave to missions. Thursday chapels were given to Mission Prayer Bands and each Band had student leadership. Students joined the Prayer Band that best represented the region of the world for which they had a special interest.

Then there was the annual Missions Convention. Leroy Lewis, Arnie Gilbertson, Barbara Gilbert, Elaine Coats, and I were the school missions officers my senior year. We had missions services every morning Monday through Friday and every evening from Monday through Thursday in the school chapel. Missionaries came and spoke to us in the chapel services. On Friday and Saturday night, we went to Fremont Tabernacle. Rev. Willard Cantelon was the speaker those two nights. Fremont Tabernacle was packed both nights. When the faith promises were calculated at the end of the week, all school records had been broken. One student gave her entire weekly check to missions during that convention. Future pastors were awakened to the need of missions and future missionaries had their calls confirmed.

My days at North Central were formative in preparation for my pastoral ministry and missionary work serving overseas. I have only good memories of those days at North Central. Lifetime friendships were established during this time of spiritual and ministerial formation. The school had a strong missions orientation, special prayer meetings, and Pentecostal outpourings. Those Pentecostal roots were evident both in the chapel services and in the classroom. I believe in North Central University. I also believe that its best days are ahead.

A Faithful Past, A Shining Future

Chapter Three

Historical Review 1955-1979

by Susan Detlefsen
Research by Hope Bahr

A Portrait of NCBI in 1955

After 25 years of operation, North Central Bible Institute proved itself as a solid and lasting member of the 11 ministerial, missionary and religious training schools of the Assemblies of God. Through the gracious support of God, institute staff, 1,400 alumni, and many supporters, NCBI survived the financial hardships of the Great Depression and the domestic challenges brought by World War II.

New financial challenges would face the Institute in the coming decades, as would the challenges of dealing with amazing growth in the student population, and finding new leadership when the Institute's founders retired and passed the torch to new leaders.

North Central continued to function under the guidance of President Frank J. Lindquist, Executive Vice President I.O. Miller and Dean T.J. Jones. The faculty consisted of servant leaders whose names would echo through Miller Hall for years to come: G. Raymond

Carlson, M.C. Nelson, Ione Soltau, Kenneth Freiheit, Arvid Kingsriter, Raymond Levang, Esther Selness, and John and Alyce Phillipps.

NCBI kept strong ties to the Minnesota District through the many district officials that served as faculty members: Treasurer Herbert Snyder, Superintendent G. Raymond Carlson, Sunday School Director E.B Adamson, and Secretary Wilson Katter.

Housed entirely in the red-brick Asbury Hospital building on the corner of 14th Street and Elliot Avenue, NCBI's modest facilities included eight classrooms; three music studios; 11 music practice rooms; 33 dormitory rooms for women and 27 rooms for men; a library; recreation and band room; cafeteria; 22 pianos, one organ and 20 typewriters. A portion of the building was used as nurse dormitories for the local hospitals until 1959.

A significant academic change in North Central's history occurred in 1955, when the Board of Directors authorized the institute to offer four-year bachelor of arts programs in theology, religious education and missions, in addition to the three-year degrees offered in these programs. The institute continued to offer a church music partnership program with the neighboring, but unaffiliated, MacPhail School of Music. Students completed their three years of study in music, and completed their fourth year at MacPhail (which is still operates in downtown Minneapolis).

Tuition cost the average student about $108 per semester, with books averaging another $20 per year. Students were allowed to work only 34 hours per week in order to keep them concentrated on their studies, but still pay their way through school.

Entrance requirements of 1955 stated that students needed a high school diploma; be at least 17 years of age; submit three character references; had a "born again" experience and experienced baptism of the Holy Spirit; baptism in water or a willingness to be; lived a life of holiness; possessed a teachable spirit; and had "obedience to a present or future call of God."

Chapter Three

Course offerings in 1955 included standards of Pentecostal higher education, such as Personal Evangelism, Homiletics, Old Testament, Greek, Sunday School Methods and Pastoral Theology. For general education courses and electives, students selected from a list that included Spanish, Typing, Logic, General Psychology, Introduction to Philosophy, First Aid, Obstetrics, Science Survey, German and others.

NCBI used mass communication for the first time to reach the community beyond its brick walls. "On Jan. 13, 1955, the school released the first of a series of telecasts over a new local station, KEYD-TV. The program, called Every Walk of Life, consists of gospel singing by students, plus a panel of faculty members who discuss pertinent questions relative to Christianity. This half hour telecast is underwritten by Northside Mercury. The entire production is under the direction of Rev. Lawrence B Larsen." (1955 *Archive*)

Intramural athletics took up some of students' time outside of the classroom. The men's basketball team was the most popular sport to either play on the court or support from the bleachers. Students often challenged each other in rousing games of table tennis, and the occasional hockey game was organized in Elliot Park.

From 1955 to 1979, the Institute acquired enough property that quadrupled the size of the campus. Enrollment continued to climb as majors and programming expanded to include more ministry and professional programs. The next two and a half decades would challenge the institute with multiple changes to the presidency. Students of many kinds would walk through the halls, sit in the classrooms and leave with God's calling on their lives.

Changing Leadership:
Presidents of North Central 1955-1979

North Central experienced the most changes in executive leadership during this period than any other. From 1955 to 1979, six different men sat behind the desk as president of the institution.

F.J. Lindquist sustained his original vision for an institute of Pentecostal higher education from the president's office until his resignation in 1961, for a total of 31 years as president. Lindquist continued to teach at North Central until his retirement in 1964.

Minnesota District Superintendent G. Raymond Carlson was selected to succeed Lindquist by the Board of Directors. A native North Dakotan, Carlson entered the position with several years of ministry leadership on his resume: executive presbyter, 13-year faculty member, pastor and district official. As one NCBC publication put it, 1961 through 1969 was "the Carlson Era."

Carlson's vision was an institution that served both those preparing for full-time ministry and for the lay servants of the church in other careers. He addressed students, "Your training at North Central Bible Institute is but a beginning. Serve God in His will whether it be as a pastor or painter, evangelist or electrician, missionary or mechanic, teacher or truck driver."

In the summer of 1969, Carlson was elected by the General Council to serve as the assistant general superintendent. He resigned the presidency of NCBC the same year.

The Rev. Cyril Homer was elected to succeed Carlson that fall. Homer assumed the position in January of 1970 and resigned six months later to accept the presidency of Southeastern College of the Assemblies of God in Lakeland, Florida.

The staff of the *Archive* wrote of Homer, "Though his stay was short, Rev. Cyril Homer's ministry at North Central touched the hearts of every student and every faculty member. He shared with us his invaluable experience as a pastor, chaplain and college president, and he presented the needs and goals of North Central Bible College throughout the United States....We said farewell with sad, but understanding hearts and with much thanksgiving to Brother Homer and his wife for their sincere dedication to God and to North Central."

Chapter Three

As the Board of Regents looked for new leadership, the Rev. D.H Mapson, Director of Development, served as interim president until the end of 1971.

As with previous presidents, the Board looked within and found a new presidential candidate, the Rev. E.M. Clark, who would serve in the position for eight years. He became the fourth president of North Central in December 1971. Like Carlson before him, Clark had served the General Council for several years as an executive presbyter, and had been a pastor and evangelist early in his ministry career. Clark was superintendent of the Illinois District when he was called by the Board of Regents.

"I shall be eternally grateful to you for encouraging me in the very first moments of my acceptance of this new responsibility," Clark wrote in his letter to the Class of 1971. Students returned that sentiment as Clark led the school through the 1970's.

"I don't think President Clark will ever realize how much we love and appreciate him. How can we express it? We can try to write it but it doesn't seem to say as much as we feel. The love and concern he has for each of us was felt the first time he spoke in chapel, and it grew. That means so much! To be loved, respected, appreciated and prayed for by the president of a college is a beautiful privilege...so to you President Clark we give much honor, love and thanks," wrote student Lynn Dexter in 1972.

Clark became chancellor of the college in 1979 and served until 1981 when he resigned and became a consultant to EMERGE Ministries in Ohio.

In 1979, Dr. Don Argue assumed the mantle of the presidency. A dean and vice president for five years at NCBC, Argue brought with him an amazing amount of experience in both ministry and non-ministry settings: pastor, evangelist, psychologist, faculty member, administrator and more. (Read more about Dr. Argue in following chapters.)

Organizational changes

A significant change to the institution occurred in 1957 when North Central Bible Institute became North Central Bible College.

The "North Central Alumni News" of summer 1957 reads, "If by chance you have not heard, your attention is called to the action of the Board of Directors of your Alma Mater – action that brought about a change of school name. The recommendation was made by the Directors to the Minnesota District Council in connection with the Annual Spring Convention that met in April in Duluth, and was approved by that body. The action did not gain approval without an objection. A school that has operated for twenty-seven years could not change a single word in its name without stirring up some nostalgia in the hearts of its graduates.

"The change was recommended because so many of the present-day applicants write to indicate their desire to attend North Central Bible College rather than North Central Bible Institute. High school counselors [sic] talk to young people about college and at times it has resulted in some confusion when it became necessary to explain that North Central Bible Institute is really a college."

Since the 1930's North Central was limited to churches and supporters in Minnesota as the Institute's sources of financial support. By invitation of the Minnesota District in the fall of 1962, the area of support grew to include the Wisconsin-Upper Michigan and South Dakota districts. In October of that year, the Board of Directors authorized the transfer of the college's title to a corporation with the membership drawn from those districts. This action gave North Central Bible College an expanded territory of operation.

"Both recruiting of students and fundraising has been enhanced by this expansion and once again North Central is moving toward the area support it enjoyed in 1930 when Wisconsin, upper Michigan, the Dakotas, and Montana were a part of North Central's home territory." (1963 *Archive*)

Chapter Three

Further expansion of North Central's support occurred in 1978 when the Regents voted to add Nebraska, Indiana, and Michigan, bringing the total number of supporting districts to eight.

The North Central campus benefited from an active Women's Auxiliary, which was started in the early 1960's. Membership included alumnae and spouses of staff and faculty members.

"We give thanks to the Ladies' Auxiliary for their thoughtfulness and expressions of love," wrote student Darcy Ready. "Their prayers, their gifts, and their concern in our behalf has been appreciated."

These dedicated women worked to furnish rooms, paint walls, provide Christmas goodies, and house students during holidays. Their sewing, cleaning, cooking and hospitality endeared these women to the student body they so diligently served.

In 1961, members of the first graduating class of 1933 met to discuss the development of alumni relations. Out of this meeting, the Alumni Association of North Central Bible College was renewed to better communicate and connect alumni from the past 30 years. The president of the association was the Rev. Amos Levang (1947). The Rev. Orill Krans (1945) led as vice president and Clara Mae Bartels (1952) served as secretary.

Academics

Over 2,000 freshmen enrolled between 1960 and 1969, with a total graduation rate of 30 percent.

"While the attrition rate may seem high...it must be remembered that unlike most other colleges, many freshmen register at North Central with the express purpose of attending but one year 'to become better rooted in the Word before entering their preferred field of study,'" wrote M.C. Nelson in 1969.

Based on graduation trends, Nelson predicted that over 700 students would graduate with degrees from NCBC during the next decade – double the previous number from the 1960's.

According to a 1972 edition of *Thrust*, the alumni newsletter, nearly 6,000 students had passed through the halls of North Central since 1930.

The year of 1974 brought a new field of study on campus to a culture that desperately needed the Gospel, the Deaf. Pioneered by the Rev. J. David Flack, the new Deaf Studies department offered a three-year diploma to prepare Deaf men and women for ministry. Courses included English, Theology classes, History of the Bible and Personal Psychology. Instructors taught Deaf students by using American Sign Language, finger spelling, voice and visual aids.

Missions and Christian Service

If NCBC students weren't in class, they were likely ministering on the streets of Minneapolis, traveling to a church on the remote North Dakota prairie, or meeting for prayer.

For decades, the student body was involved in "missionary bands," clubs that met weekly to become better acquainted with customs, needs, and prayer requests of various countries and the missionaries who served there. "The ultimate purpose in having this knowledge before us is to bring us to a place of deeper realization of our part in this great work," wrote one student.

Students showed their support in financial gifts as well. "We count our missionary convention of this year as a great success. Not only were some called to dedicate their lives as missionaries in a foreign field but all were moved to give sacrificially of their time and money..." the editorial team of the *Archive* recorded. According to the 1955 *Archive*, NCBI was first among the Assemblies of God schools in per capita giving and second in total giving.

"The missionary conventions the past three years have been a time of great spiritual awakening. The daily feasts on God's Word will long be remembered," wrote one student in the 1956 *Archive*. That year, guest missionary and alumna Palma Ramsborg visited the campus to describe her work in Formosa, China, and India.

Chapter Three

"The spiritual tide of the school this year is very high. We felt the presence of God during the revival when the Spirit fell and many were filled with the Holy Spirit, and others refilled," testified another student.

In the 1960's, students participated in ministry and volunteer work at different local churches through the Christian Service Training program.

The prayer bands and Christian Service department were amended as time passed, but student passion for and involvement in the groups didn't change.

Students participated in the Student Missionary Society that met weekly at chapel services to pray for different mission fields supported by Assemblies of God.

"Being on the Missions Staff is exciting! It gives those of us on the staff experience in aspects of Christian Service we will encounter later in ministry. That's valuable!" wrote Chuck Lamson, student missions president of 1972. "As far as present school life is concerned, Missions Staff work provides opportunities for us to be involved in campus activities and to become better acquainted with fellow students. Learning spiritual responsibilities in Christian leadership is one of the greatest values of participation in the missions program at North Central. Here we learn to put 'feet' on the Great Commission and 'heart' into our prayers for a harvest of souls."

"Being prayer band president can mean sitting up all Wednesday night searching desk drawers for interesting slides, asking someone at 11 p.m. to tell what 'missions' means to him, and baking 100 cookies to draw sleepy, hungry students into a certain room for 45 minutes," wrote Diane Sundell, president of the Latin America prayer band in 1973. "I have found that it can also be an opportunity to stir up and intensify in a group of young people a burden for reaching lost souls; it can be the challenge to make missions, missionaries, and mission fields real subjects for everyone's prayers.

But most of all, it does mean bringing our burden for missions home and reaching out to those around us that have not encountered Christ."

The power of mass communication found a new niche in the "I found it!" campaign, which North Central students took part in during 1977. The evangelism campaign, started in 1976 by a pastoral fellowship in Georgia, managed to spread to Minnesota. Students used bumper stickers, buttons, stickers, yard signs and other means to prompt passersby to ask, "What did you find?"

Students took to the streets in the Midwest and elsewhere during this period of history. Students took part in Operation Outreach, a ministry movement in which student teams "invaded" 44 Iowa churches on Oct. 20, 1967 and integrated with church staff, leading Sunday school classes, performing special music numbers, and making rest home visitation trips. The trip gave students chances to serve the churches and publicize the college.

Also that year, students took trips to Superior, Wisconsin and Lexington, Minnesota, where they canvassed neighborhoods with the gospel, gave out literature and held rallies. Their work resulted in over 100 decisions for salvation.

The 1968 *Archive* notes that during the summer, students were involved in a Teen Challenge ministry in the Philadelphia area, ministering to "Hippies and drug addicts" at a coffee shop called "Hidden Manna," as well as street preaching, door to door canvassing and visits to churches. In Minneapolis, a street witnessing program involved 30 students who actively worked in the downtown area and the nearby University of Minnesota campus.

Student Activities

Student publications were a staple of campus communication throughout NCBC's history. During the 1950's, *The Archette* published snippets of news for students. Then, in 1960, *The Northern*

Chapter Three

Light was published as a student-produced publication in newspaper format. Past editors of *The Northern Light* during this period included David Koechel, Jim Bakker, and Rocky Grams.

"Why *The Northern Light?*" wrote 1973 editor Rocky Grams. "When the year began, we felt there should be a paper because 'every other decent college has one, so why shouldn't we?' Of course, in the back of our minds were vague notions of the need for news and also a desire to help kids want to stay here and fulfill their calling....Since then we've aged (not to say matured) a little and our ideals have too. As we look forward to next year, we'd like the paper to become less and less of an image-builder or a joke sheet and become more of a vehicle of awareness, a catalyst of thought and an inspiration to action."

Although they might not have known it, the staff of the *Archive*, North Central's yearbook, faithfully chronicled volumes of history that have become an invaluable link to the college's past. Almost every year was recorded by the student photographers, writers and editors of the yearbook staff into a priceless volume of NCBC history.

In 1962, North Central was part of the Minnesota River Athletic Conference, and the men's teams competed with other colleges in baseball and basketball. Ten years later, the college would offer men's teams in baseball, tennis, and basketball, with the basketball team defeating three local colleges in NCBC's conference to become conference champs in 1972. The women's cheerleading squad kept the crowd involved from the sidelines.

Near the end of the 1970's, the North Central "Chiefs" had varsity basketball and baseball teams that played in local conferences. A club softball team for women, the "Chiefettes," was also active.

Annual spring banquets encouraged formal attire and civil behavior from students at least once a year. Spring picnics brought students out into Elliot Park or Como Park for a picnic lunch, silly games, softball tournaments and the occasional "Dunk the Prof" contest. Homecoming events were held every year as well, including a banquet and coronation of royalty.

As with past years, student singing groups and drama teams traveled across the member districts to minister with their talents and publicize the work of North Central Bible College. The many groups throughout the years included the Songfellows, the Master's Melodettes, Harvest Time Trio, the Choralettes, Gospel Flames, the Gospel Gleaners, Psalmsters, Galileans, Revivalaires, Judeans, Redemption, and Liberty.

North Central's campus retained a culturally conservative atmosphere throughout two decades that were known afterward as periods of dramatic cultural upheaval. Despite these changes, North Central maintained a formal dress code for men and women both on and off campus. Dresses and skirts were required for the ladies, as were coats and ties for the men. Blue jeans, overalls and "painter pants" were not allowed on either men or women. "All male students are expected to be cleanly shaven and refrain from beards or extreme hair styles," was the mandate from the 1979 student life handbook. Students were also required to refrain from going to movie theaters, a form of entertainment "which tends to compromise our testimony as leaders in the church of Jesus Christ."

Physical Growth and Expansion

North Central University would be blessed with the acquisition of several properties during the next two decades.

In 1966, NCBC purchased property and apartment buildings on 9th street, where Phillipps Hall now stands.

In August of 1969, NCBC took possession of the Asbury Hospital building adjacent to the campus on 15th Street, and the Tourtellotte Home. Before the purchase, both buildings were in use by the Methodist denomination as hospital facilities and a retirement home.

Known at first as the Men's Residence, the hospital building was

Chapter Three

later rededicated as G. Raymond Carlson Hall. The lower floor was retained as a food service venue while the upper floors were used as dormitory rooms for over 200 students.

The Tourtellotte Home was originally built in 1913 and redesigned for the housing and training of deaconesses of the Methodist Church in the years following World War II. Mrs. Harriet Arnold Tourtellotte had the building built in memory of her husband, Dr. Jacob F. Tourtellotte, a Navy surgeon and Minneapolis land owner. Nurses and students began to live in the building in 1946. In 1961, the building was restored and then became a home for retired hospital workers.

North Central Bible College purchased the Tourtellotte building on December 24, 1968. For a time, the facility was known as the Tourtellotte Guest Center, and then it was remodeled in 1973 and turned into the T.J. Jones Memorial Library; the Library's original collection totaled over 20,000 books.

At the end of the 1970's North Central's Board of Regents had approved plans for the College Life Center, a new building complex adjacent to the Lindquist Chapel building that would include classrooms, administrative offices and, most anticipated by the students, an indoor gymnasium.

After 40 years, one of North Central's most recognizable buildings was rededicated and renamed. During the 1978 baccalaureate service, an announcement was made that the red-brick administration building at 910 Elliot Avenue would be named Ivan O. Miller Hall, after the first vice president of the college. I.O. Miller resigned from the vice presidency in 1961 after serving as a faculty member and administrator for 25 years. He noted that his failing health was keeping him from "serv[ing] the school in the way I believe it should be served." His resignation was refused twice by the administration before they finally accepted.

Earlier, Miller recalled that when North Central purchased the

Asbury hospital building, some naysayers exclaimed, "We couldn't operate this if it were given to us." Seventy years later, it can be said with certainty that those people were wrong.

Construction of the F.J. Lindquist Chapel

Since its founding, North Central's ministry and worship nexus had always been its chapel program. While the frequency and duration of chapel services fluctuated over the years as determined by the leadership, these services brought students, faculty and staff together for communal worship, prayer and seeking after the heart and mind of God.

A separate chapel building, designed specifically as a chapel venue, became an urgent need in the late 1960's. The growth of the student body had stressed the chapel room in Miller Hall to the limit. "We have placed extra chairs in every possible space, yet there isn't enough space for every student," said D.H. Mapson, Director of Development, in 1970.

The original chapel project was titled "Project 71" after the proposed completion date for the chapel. The college leadership planned to construct a combined chapel and auditorium building that could seat over 2,000 people before the end of 1971. Plans called for closing Elliot Avenue, which was NCBC property, and building the auditorium next to the recently acquired Men's Residence building and Tourtellotte Guest Center.

In 1971, the architectural plans changed. The building was moved across Elliot Avenue, and the auditorium was scaled back to a more modest number of 1,000 seats. The Board approved the plans and, as funds continued to gather for the building, building contracts were signed.

President Clark's 1972 appeal to alumni for support stated, "the giving exceeded anything any of us had ever seen, until there is presently a total of $130,000 in the Chapel Fund. This has been given

Chapter Three

since seven months ago. We only lack $95,000 to completely pay for the chapel. We are trusting God for this amount to come in."

Students took the fundraising for the new chapel to heart. Spiritual Emphasis week in 1972 kindled a spirit of giving in numerous students. Many sold television sets, stereos, and even their cars in order to support the building. Over $25,000 was raised by the student body alone toward the building fund.

Construction of the chapel building was completed in 1973. "The new chapel seats a total of 950, 600 on the first floor and 350 in the balcony. The architect is Richard Vanman...of Vanman Construction Co...The exterior is brick with a brick interior, a completely carpeted sloping floor, pews and air conditioning" (1973 *Archive*).

The next 30 years of chapel services, altar time, concerts and movings of the Spirit in this building stood out in the minds of alumni as life-changing experiences. The Lindquist Chapel truly became the heart of the North Central campus.

In 1974 President Clark wrote, "We have shared a miracle in that this is the first year we have used the new chapel. We hadn't realized what a difference it would make. It has been hallowed by the sacrifices of the many, many people who have helped make it possible. It seems as if the presence of the Lord is always there."

Some of the people who made a difference

1930-61 – Rev. F.J. Lindquist, President, founder

1930-61 – Rev. Ivan O. Miller, Executive Vice-President

1955 – Rev. W.A. Katter, Secretary

1955-1961 – Rev. W. R. Snyder, Treasurer

1946 – Rev. T.J. Jones, Faculty member and Dean of North Central

1950 – Rev. Arvid Kingsriter, Faculty member, director of Public Relations

1949 – Rev. John P. Phillipps, Faculty member, administrator

1948 – Miss Ione Soltau, Dean of Women
1969 – R.R. Bayless, Dean of students, counselor
1951 – R.K. Levang – faculty member
1978 – William R. Brookman, faculty member
1974 – Joanne Kersten, faculty member

Chapter Four

Alumni Memories 1955-1979

Faithful Giving and Miracles
Rev. E.M. Clark, fourth president of North Central Bible College

E.M. Clark remembers that North Central was blessed by God with faithful giving and faithful administrators and students during his tenure, which made the construction of the F.J. Lindquist Chapel and Clark-Danielson College Life Center possible.

We arrived in Minneapolis just in time to start the second semester in January 1971.

The Business Manager took me to meet the president of the bank with which the college did business. He said the operation of the college must improve if the college was to continue to do business with the bank and asked for a monthly report on progress.

We spoke on "Giving" in the chapel services that semester and took pledges from just the student body and the faculty. My wife, who was the bookkeeper in our family, said we were $100 short per month on our budget for the year, but we pledged $100 per month by faith for the year. The response was very good from faculty and students.

At Partners For Progress that year, people were also very generous. That year $232,000 came in offerings and payments on pledges. I was told that the previous record for giving in one year was $75,000!

In the summer of 1971, Richard Vanman, our building contractor and architect, asked me if he could give money from the sale of a property he owned to start a fund to build a new chapel. It was needed badly. I told him that would be great, but I knew that money was very scarce at that time.

Revival came that fall. Richard Vanman gave $40,000, and Gunnar Danielson gave the same. Both of them gave without being asked to give. We pledged what seemed impossible to us – $1,000.

Students got excited about a new chapel, and many of them gave everything they had to the new building – a total of $25,000. We couldn't borrow any money for it, since there was a mortgage on the land. A friend gave us $100,000. He said, "This is not a loan; if you need it, use it. But if not, of course you can give it back."

The money came in, so we gave the $100,000 back to the friend. The fall months of 1971 were a time of real revival in the whole operation. In the fall of 1972, we dedicated the F.J. Lindquist Chapel, the first new building ever built on the campus, debt free. There was great rejoicing because of God's goodness and the kindness and generosity of friends of the college.

Gary Grogan's wedding was the first wedding in the new Chapel. We were good friends before that and we still communicate.

I loved the student body. The students all felt free to come and see me in my office. Many left "love notes" on my desk at night. I always had a good relationship with the majority of the student body. I have always loved young people and have always wanted to help them in any way that I could. They seemed to feel free to talk to me about falling in love and getting married.

Mike Shields and Mona Grams were in love and planning to be married. She graduated one year before him. She planned to leave and go on the mission field. I suggested that she stay there and be busy at something else until he graduated, since I had a bit of experience in that field. She stayed, and they have had a beautiful life together.

When Brother [G. Raymond] Carlson told me he had had a revelation that I was to take the job as president of the college [after Cyril Homer], I was afraid to say yes. I felt I was not prepared for such an important undertaking. But when the board told me "I was missing God," I really prayed about it.

I asked God to give me a scripture when I opened the Bible that would make it clear what I was to do. After prayer, I opened the Bible where it seemed to want to open. It opened to the prophet Elijah talking to God when the Brook Kerith had gone dry. God said, "Get thee to Zarephath. I have caused a widow woman to sustain thee there." Only He emphasized that *He* would sustain me.

At the end of the spring semester in 1971, the business manager resigned and left the college. His bookkeeper told me that the bills were five months behind; the line of credit at the bank was spent. We needed $25,000 within the next two weeks, and $30,000 at the first of the month, plus money to operate through the summer. I was tempted to be discouraged, but God reminded me of His promise to sustain me.

That weekend while I was attending my home church, pastored by Arvid Kingsriter, a young lady handed me an envelope at the close of the service. It had writing on it that ended with, "Thus saith the Lord." I didn't know her, and she said later that she never knew me and was starting to give a prophecy, but God stopped her and impressed her to write it out and pointed me out as the one who should have it. She said she didn't know me or what I did. I put the envelope in my shirt pocket.

A Faithful Past, A Shining Future

When I got home, I took the envelope out and read the writing on it: "Do not be discouraged, for have I not proven myself to you many, many times? Be not afraid, for I will not fail you, and I will keep my promise unto you, thus saith the Lord."

Here was a reminder of the promise God had made to me when I decided to "go there."

There was not one embarrassment over the lack of money as long as I was at North Central. How could anyone refuse to obey a God as loving and kind as that?!

More changes were happening outside the college that affected it internally.

The city would not allow us to build more buildings without added parking. So, with the consent of the donors, we used the money to build parking ramps on Elliot Ave and 10th Ave. Then the Minnesota District purchased new property to serve as their headquarters and moved out of the offices on campus. This gave us more room for expansion.

The president of the bank called and asked me and the new business manager to have lunch with him. At lunch he said he liked the way I did business. He then offered to almost quadruple the college's line of credit, with the option to borrow even more from sister banks if the need arose. I told him we really didn't need that much, but we appreciated his kindness.

I was speaking in one of the churches in Illinois one Sunday. I had helped them build their church while I was superintendent in Illinois. At the close of the evening service, when I stepped away from the pulpit to turn the service back to the pastor, his wife stepped up to the microphone and said, "Brother Clark, the gift of the word of knowledge is now in operation. You have a dream that has not been fulfilled. I think it is a building at the college. In a few days, a key man will come to the college. Listen to him, and it will be done."

On Tuesday of the following week, Gunnar Danielson called and

Chapter Four

wanted to have the builder Dick Vanman and I meet him for lunch. He told us that God had given him a vision in his sleep about building the new administration building. The two men agreed that they would each give $100,000 to the project and that Gunnar would raise the money to pay for the rest of it without any cost to the college.

When Don Argue became our dean, he really smoothed out the way for us in those areas. He did a very good job, and after several years I felt very relieved to turn the college over to him. I was glad to recommend him to the Board for the presidency when I felt that my work was done. I left NCBC in 1981 before the total completion of the buildings, but Dr. Argue was able to complete the work that had been started. I worked hard but I learned some things that were very important to my future.

I met two great men who set an example of faith that motivated other people to give so generously that new buildings began to spring up to bless the people of the college. Their example caused others to learn to give when God impressed them to give amounts that seemed utterly impossible. I myself learned that nothing is impossible if it is in God's will.

God has been very gracious to me. I have been able to work to 90 years of age and do some writing even since that time. I thank Him for what hard work He has given me to do, for I feel that I have been more than repaid for all I have ever done for the enlargement of the Kingdom of God.

The Impact a Professor Can Make

Interview of Tom Hartwell
by Bethany Moeller, North Central University student

Tom Hartwell graduated from North Central Bible College in

1964 with a Bachelor of Arts in Bible and Theology. He was vice president of the student body for a year, president of his senior class, and president of the Homeland and North American Indians prayer bands. During his time as a student, Hartwell found himself more than occupied preaching on the weekends. He still managed time to enjoy playing basketball on the college team. Before North Central had its own gymnasium, Hartwell played intramural basketball in a city league.

Many professors and staff members impacted Tom's life during his Bible college days and helped mold him into the person he became. He remembers that T.J. Jones offered him tremendous inspiration from the Bible in classes such as Old Testament, one of Hartwell's favorite classes. New Testament class was another, taught by Arvid Kingsriter. Ray Levang, John Phillipps, and G. Raymond Carlson were more professors who became some of Hartwell's dearest friends and helped guide him in his life of ministry.

Hartwell said, "I honestly cannot think of a single teacher or staff member at North Central who left a negative impression on me...The last time I visited NCU, there is such growth in the college, but the same objectives and presence of the Lord are still there, and that's such an encouragement to me." Hartwell testifies of North Central's vital role in impacting his life, commenting of the school.

"I can't say enough good things about it!"

Those Musical Groups

Interview of Ronna Wyant
by NCU Student Calley Donath

Ronna (Wiley) Wyant, currently of New Brighton, tells us that traveling music groups were a big part of North Central's ministry

Chapter Four

during the 1960's. Groups such as the Galileans, the Choralettes, and the Gospel Keynotes were among the ensembles that traveled around Minnesota and nearby states on the weekends and during the summers. These groups consisted of three to four members, either coed or girls only. Voice and piano were the instruments of choice during this time.

As a "pastor's kid" or PK, ministry was in Ronna Wyant's blood. She became involved with these teams as soon as she arrived at North Central and has been involved with music ministry in various settings ever since. Also, Ronna worked on the 1960 *Archive* yearbook during her freshman year.

Ronna served as a secretary for Oral Krans and also served as the accompanist for his choir, The Choralettes. In 1964, Krans handed the leadership of the choir to Wyant, which she directed for a year. "Oral Krans gave me immeasurable guidance in my formative years. He was a wonderful example of commitment, both to work and to the Lord," Ronna says. She taught at North Central from 1967 through 1970.

A Trip and Intercession

Interview of Charles and Myrna Skaggs
by Calley Donath, North Central University student

Charles Skaggs was living in Wisconsin when he was called to North Central. His father was the minister at a church in La Crosse. During one Sunday night service Charles was at the altar spending time with God. When he finally opened his eyes, he found himself alone at the altar with his father. After that evening, he knew that he was called to be in the ministry and that he was to attend North Central.

One of the professors he remembered at North Central was T.J. Jones, a Bible teacher with "a love for the word of God and an insistence on getting his students' priorities straight." Jones used to say that students needed to get "books, Buick, and bride." Skaggs got all three, except he got a Chevrolet instead of a Buick.

Skaggs remembers his time as a student when the college was in a transition of leadership. "All of the founders of North Central were passing the torch on to other leaders," including the retirement of Frank Lindquist and Ivan Miller.

During one particular Spiritual Emphasis week, Charles remembers "such a huge spirit of giving that people started signing over their paychecks. Someone presented a great need and students who worked for $1 to $1.10 an hour were dedicating thousands of dollars to the building need. Some students were even giving the pink slips of their cars; it was a way they knew that only God could be in control of something so remarkable."

The nightly curfews of 11 p.m. on weekdays and midnight on weekends weren't hard to adhere to, but wearing ties and sports jackets to class was a big deal. Skaggs remembers a group of guys who thought that they could make a protest by just not wearing the right clothes. So, a bunch of these guys just wore sweaters to class, but they were immediately sent back to their dorms to change.

Skaggs was highly involved in the music at North Central. He was in choir and various other music groups including mixed quartet and male quartet. One group was called the "Crusaders." He was actively involved in music ministry and youth groups in the Minneapolis area. His male quartet frequently toured the Twin Cities area, and "we thought we were really something."

He met his wife, Myrna, at a Bible family camp in Wisconsin through singing. She also attended North Central and was a Music major.

"Altogether North Central days were some of the best, because it

Chapter Four

was the time I was being poured into. I was dating my future wife, and I was making lifelong friends who were learning to serve in the kingdom of God."

Myrna Skaggs remembers Jim and Tammy Bakker as students while she was also a student. When Tammy came to school, she was going out with another guy. She lived on the fifth floor of Miller Hall with Myrna.

The girls on that floor where continually doing pranks in the bathroom, like putting Saran Wrap over the toilets or garbage by the doors. She lived right by the bathroom, so she was always waking up to laughter and giggles.

Some of the professors she remembers are Ray Levang, who came from her hometown in Wisconsin. He taught a science class that made science seem interesting, which she appreciated because science was a subject she didn't care for very much.

She also remembers music teacher L.B. Larsen, since she was a music major. She and her friends, Ronna and Donna (and her name Myrna—which all rhymed) played in different groups. She played in the school choir, the Evangelaires. Larson would never let them all play together because he would say there was "too much talent." Lowell Lundstrum wrote a lot of music and songs, and Myrna often arranged the music for him.

Myrna was in an outreach group that went to places around Minneapolis, but once they went all the way to Winnipeg. The school administrators didn't want the group to go because it was winter and the roads were bad. However, the three men and three women went and on the way back they slid on slippery roads and hit a pole going 55 miles per hour.

One woman was flung out of the car and was injured badly. Her leg looked like it had been folded back, and Myrna thought that the girl's leg would have to be "taken off." While she was walking back from the hospital through Elliot Park, she couldn't stop crying because of the emotional drain and worry. She found out later that her mother had woken up in the middle of the night at the exact time of the accident and had been interceding in prayer for them. In time, the injured woman recovered, and her leg healed.

Charles Skaggs is currently a chaplain in the jails near Moreno Valley, California. He graduated from NCBC in 1965.

What's 'Caught'

Interview of Pastor Ron and Margo Traub
by Ashley Cole, North Central University student

As a young boy, Ron Traub had the call of God on his life. He knew that he was going to go to Bible school and into the ministry. When the men's trio from North Central came to his church, that was the deciding factor. The group of men went out for pizza with the youth group, and they encouraged Ron to come to North Central.

Margo attended one year. Her parents wanted all their children to spend at least a year at North Central. However, out of four children, only Margo and her brother attended.

Missions

Missions and prayer bands were a big focus at North Central during the Traubs' time. Every student would be in a mission band. Their duties included praying for a particular country and contacting the missionaries serving there. Missions conventions were held annually, and particular mission bands would go up in front and report on their countries. For one missions convention, Margo dressed up as a little Chinese girl at her booth, and no one could tell it was her. It was one of the highlights of her life, and missions became a big part of the Traubs' life.

Chapter Four

Ron remembered a specific missions convention when the sense to give was heavy. In one of the offerings, Ron felt impressed to give everything that he had, which was $5. So he gave it, and later he found a $10 check in his mailbox from a member of his church back home. It was the only letter that this member sent him the entire time while Ron was at North Central. It was highly impressed upon Ron that God would take care of him and that a giving heart is what God wants the most.

Rebels

The dress code mandated that women couldn't wear slacks, shorts, or short skirts. The men had to wear shirts and ties. Margo used to wear short skirts and put a long jacket over them!

Students couldn't get engaged, get married or date without getting permission from the dean. The front door was locked at 11 p.m. – midnight on the weekends. If a student was late, they would get written up. However, according to Margo, if you brought a wire hanger you could pick the lock and get in. It was very much like camp, and you had to be in your room with hallway lights out. You couldn't have any electrical appliances, so several people put their food outside the windows to keep it cold.

Meetings

The best social gatherings of the winter took place on the ice rink at Elliot Park. The park was flooded and after the water froze everyone would go ice skating. Ron and Margo were first introduced at the Elliot Park rink. Ron came in the middle of the year when both he and Margo were freshmen. Ron first saw Margo stepping off the elevator. He had to ask several people who the "foxy" red-head was, and they were introduced as they were ice skating. However, Margo had a different boyfriend. He ended up making a lot of money, but she is glad that she didn't end up marrying him.

Margo went to youth camp and was a roommate with Tammy Faye Bakker, and they attended North Central at the same time; however, both she and Jim were a year older. Jim was from Michigan (same state as Ron), so Ron knew him from Michigan camps.

Learning

According to Ron, a student's performance in Greek class was the deciding factor that determined if you had what it took to be in college. He and Clarence St. John were the youngest members of the class and were mocked by the older students. This only bolstered Traub's and St. John's determination to get an A in Greek, so much so that they studied during their jobs at Sears. They kept each other accountable. When they both received A's, they astonished the faculty and the rest of the class.

The whole time Ron was at North Central he had a full-time job and left college debt free. He was paid more while he attended North Central than his first four years in the ministry. He was a janitor at Sears' upper floor offices from 3 p.m. till 12. Margo was a nurse's assistant at Northwestern, and she worked the night shift full time from 11 p.m. to 7 a.m.

Caught

"There was so much taught at North Central, but what was important and life changing was the stuff that was caught. A lot of the lifelong lessons were not paid for in tuition."

The importance of a network of friends was one of the most valuable lessons. The Traubs enjoy looking back now at the associates in ministry all over the world, whom the Traubs love to visit and catch up with. The kinship born in those days has survived a variety of experiences. Friends are some of the best things that were gained from their North Central experience.

Chapter Four

Margo and Ron have both taken much from North Central. "The biggest things gained at North Central is the stuff that isn't part of the curriculum," say the Traubs. "It is the time of prayer at the altar, the friends gained, and the sense of God in life. For many it is the first time away from home, and they are beginning to make life decisions. North Central is a safe place to make those while finding God's direction. This is something you don't find in the catalog."

Margo and Ron Traub are pastors at Sioux Falls, South Dakota. Ron Traub is the current Chairman of the Board of Regents at North Central University.

Our Memories of Our Years at NCBC

Dan and Nancy Rector

Nancy Rector

I attended Bethany AG in Adrian, Michigan as a teenager. I gave my heart to the Lord after hearing the Rev. Art Clay preach. I felt that I was the only person in the sanctuary that evening and that he was talking just to me. I was raised in a Congregational church and I had never heard the plan of salvation and I didn't know that I needed to ask Jesus into my life. That was the beginning of a new path for me, and when my friend Faye Poe asked me if I wanted to go to college with her, I said yes. I knew nothing about North Central. I was raised on a farm and very involved in 4-H and I was used to going to Michigan State University (a campus of hundreds of acres and lots of buildings) for many events. So the first time I saw the one building (Miller Hall) of North Central Bible College, I was in total shock. I couldn't believe that I would be living, eating meals, attending classes, and everything else in this one building, but it began to feel like home in a matter of weeks.

My roommates were Faye (Poe) Slaybaugh and Karen (Peterson) Booher. In high school, I was involved on the yearbook staff and really loved photography and layout work, and so at North Central, I got involved on the yearbook staff taking many of the photos in the 1966-67 yearbook.

I started dating Dan Rector, and we were engaged in the spring of 1967. We were married on August 19, 1967. Once again, Faye was instrumental in an important event in my life as she was the one who introduced Dan to me. She knew him from his years on the radio show "Children's Bible Hour" and when he would sing at family camp at Fa Ho Lo Park Camp at Grass Lake, Michigan.

After our marriage, I worked while Dan finished his last two years at NCBC. We lived at 1420 Portland Avenue in a furnished apartment for $80 a month for rent. We left NCBC debt free. Just before we left Minneapolis, work was beginning on 35W freeway behind our apartment building.

Dan started teaching part time at North Central in 1978. In 1990 he joined the full-time faculty. During those years, I took occasional classes and just plodded along slowly earning a degree. In 1990, I looked at my transcript and realized that I was close to getting my degree, so I went full time and graduated in 2001 with a B.S. degree in Psychology, and I was granted a minor in Children's Ministries.

Dan Rector

I came to NCBC in the fall of 1965 from Grand Rapids, Michigan, with a call to ministry on my life. I had heard about North Central for many years since I was brought up in the AG. Also, two of my aunts had attended NCBI in the 1930's. I had a strong music background so the excellent music program at North Central was also one of the reasons for my choice. I did not decide until after school started in my freshman year whether I would be a pastoral major or a music major. I chose pastoral but was very involved in the music programs through my years as a student. I sang in the Evangelaires for two years and also in a gospel quartet. I also wrote the theme chorus for the Missions Convention my senior year.

In 1978, while on staff at Bloomington Assembly of God, I started teaching Children's Ministry classes at North Central. At that time, I did not realize that I was creating a new job for myself. Children's Ministries became a major at the school in 1988 and I joined the full-time faculty to head the program in 1990. During these years, Children's Ministries graduates have become some of the most sought after graduates from NCU.

Shared memories

President G. Raymond Carlson was the neatest man I have ever met. He knew everyone by name and he would call you by name every time he saw you in the halls. I knew I was special when he talked to me. He was as much like Christ as anyone I have ever known. He and his beloved Mae sent Christmas cards to us every year until his death, and she continued until her health kept her from it.

Rev. Don Tanner was a wonderful teacher, friend and mentor to both of us. He was great in the classroom, and we really learned a lot from his teaching. He was the music director at our church, Bloomington AG and he would have us sing often in the services.

Dr. John Phillipps was a great teacher and friend also. He attended Bloomington AG with us, and he called us "Dapper Dan and Fancy Nancy." He was such a humble man and he was always willing and eager to make others feel important. He had a great gift of love, and he shared it with us freely.

The Missions convention was a special time at NCBC and all of the "prayer bands" worked very hard on huge displays of their countries to put on the walls of the chapel. (The chapel was the room behind the elevator that is now Elementary Education Lab.) We were in the Latin American Prayer Band, and Ken Dahlagher was the president.

Fern Olson was one of the many speakers in chapel and when she spoke on the Baptism of the Holy Spirit, Nancy received it with the evidence of speaking in tongues for the first time. It was great!

George Rasmussen was the person who ran the bookstore and he became a favorite of mine. He was very funny, but I knew that he cared for me and would be the first to pray for me in a crisis. He was a good friend for many, many years.

I remember that we were seated in chapel in alphabetical order, so Nancy got to sit on the front row because her last name started with a "B." I was near the back of the long and narrow room.

The cafeteria was down on the north end of first floor where the Registrar's Office is now. The piano practice rooms were in the basement and were a great place to meet a special person for a date.

We were assigned churches to attend on Sundays. Nancy attended Anoka AG and it took hours to get there via the old back roads. There were no highways back then, so when we finally got back to school, it was very late at night. I went to Mount Olivet AG in Apple Valley and it was the same for me. The roads were single lane with the one-way bridge over the Minnesota River. We really enjoyed the services and our involvement in these churches.

In the 1960's, the music programs were excellent. The Evangelaires choir was a large mixed choir and they traveled extensively and promoted the school. Dan was in this group. L.B. Larson was the director and he was a master at getting the best performance out of his choir. They also sang on T.V. and did a Christmas concert at Southdale Mall in 1966.

The Gospel Hymns was a very sharp men's group that traveled and ministered in many churches throughout the Midwest.

Chapter Four

The Choralettes was the girls choir and Dallas Holm was the soloist. Nancy was in this group during a tour in the spring of 1967 through Wisconsin, Illinois, Indiana, Ohio and Michigan.

Nancy (Barrow) Rector was a student from 1966 to 1967, and then returned to finish her degree from 1992 to 2001. She is the wife of Dan Rector, alumnus of North Central (Class of 1969) and faculty member in 1978. Dan currently serves as North Central's Children's Ministry Specialist.

A View of NCBC In Its Fifth Decade

Mike Shields
Missionary evangelist to Latin America

North Central was in a crisis in the fall of 1970 when I showed up as a new freshman student. Our President, Cy Homer, had served for less than a year when he was asked to go to Florida in an urgent attempt to stabilize a difficult, crisis situation at Southeastern Bible College. By the time I arrived in August of that year, North Central was without its principal leader, and the institution hit an emotional rock bottom.

There was a clear sense of alarm my first semester concerning the school's finances and its very survival. The student body was small that year, numbering only about 400. We were urged to turn off the lights at every opportunity and sternly warned not to waste paper towels and toilet paper. That was really hard for rowdy upperclassmen who needed vast supplies of TP for regular thud-bomb raids.

Coming from Iowa, I was stunned people would do something like that. Back in Goose Lake, high-grade toilet paper could be traded for valuable things like 8-track tapes and fishing tackle.

A Faithful Past, A Shining Future

During registration I gasped in the Accounting Office to find out classes would cost a whopping $17.50 per credit hour. They assured me we were fortunate that semester; it would leap to $19 by January. The message was, "Pay up. Be thankful."

I dutifully signed for a National Defense Student Loan. I never quite figured out how I was defending the nation by incurring debt. Today, it seems a lot of people must be defending the nation with MasterCard, Visa, and American Express. Yet, it made me feel patriotic during the Vietnam War. Too young to go fight, at least I could incur some debt and attend Bible college.

The NDSL loan covered my first semester expenses: $280 housing, $210 for four classes, and roughly a hundred bucks in fees. I was overwhelmed that afternoon in late August 1970 at borrowing $700. Yet, this was Minneapolis. You could make a lot more money here than back on the farm. Within a week I was working at a gas station three blocks from the college earning $2 an hour. With money flowing like that, I knew it wouldn't take more than a year to pay off my debt. I missed the calculation by 13 years.

The harrowing financial situation of the college back in the early 1970's could have been the death knell for the institution. During the transitions from G. Raymond Carlson to Cy Homer and E. M. Clark, there was a key man who provided rock solid stability and quiet leadership. That man was the Rev. Marvin C. Nelson.

M.C. (as he was affectionately called by just about everyone outside of the classroom) was a man of unusual personal discipline. Tall, wiry, strong, mild-mannered, and brilliant, he was the quintessential mix of educator, leader and athlete. A long distance runner, he often tried to get me to go on his 5 a.m. five mile runs in the 20-below weather of Minnesota. When I finally agreed to go to his house and join him for a run, I convinced him it would be better for me to slowly drive with the lights on to protect him from cars on the isolated road. None came.

Chapter Four

M.C. Nelson was the academic dean of North Central for over 20 years. He had a distinguished military service record, serving with distinction as a chaplain with the U.S. Army in Europe during World War II. He was in the active reserves the entire time he served at North Central. Several times he took me on weekend visits to various locations to hold services for the reservists. He held the rank of lieutenant colonel and was highly respected by the officers everywhere we went. In his full dress uniform with gold leaf insignia and impressive epaulets, Lt. Colonel Nelson was the pride of North Central. M.C. was always proud he was still able to fit into the uniform he wore for his wedding.

M.C. Nelson was the professor at North Central with a master's degree, the highest academic degree in the college. Because of his educational background and military service, he had been admitted to the University of Minnesota master's program in communications. M.C. did very well in his program. He later leveraged his academic standing to boost North Central's credentials among his educational peers in other Twin Cities institutions. A few years after he finished his degree, he used his influence and military credentials to get yet another North Central grad into the same U of M program. That young man was admitted only on the stipulation that he would maintain straight A's in every class. Monroe Grams, my father-in-law, did just that. Because of M.C. Nelson and Monroe Grams, North Central was established as a place producing quality people capable of competing at the highest academic levels. The relationships established with the U of M and the demonstration of high capability set the stage for the eventual accreditation of North Central University.

Anyone who attended North Central during our years will remember M.C. Nelson stepping to the pulpit in the small, second-floor chapel in what is known today as Miller Hall. Standing tall and confident, he launched into a memorized, brilliantly-delivered rendition of the third chapter of Colossians. His recitation would approach the end with a powerful anointing that caused praises to rise up among students and faculty alike. It was one of the most inspiring things I ever saw in a North Central Chapel service as a student.

M.C. Nelson was married with three children. Sadly, his 20-year-old son turned away from the Lord. The boy was involved in a jewelry store robbery in downtown St. Paul in 1972. In a struggle with a police officer, the gun discharged and M.C.'s son was killed instantly. Many times I stopped in to visit M.C. at his office, comforting him in my own simple way. I was a 19-year-old student unskilled in anything other than love and admiration for a man who grieved in private over a lost son whom he loved so much.

On the day Mona and I married, the Rev. M.C. Nelson stood on the platform of the Minneapolis Gospel Tabernacle with his friend, the Rev. Monroe Grams. They married us in 1973. M.C. became like a second dad to both of us, visiting us in Marshall, Minnesota where we pastored our first church, and going along with us to General Council in Denver, Colorado in 1975.

In August 1977, we were excited to go again with M.C. to General Council. We had rooms reserved in Oklahoma City. Always ahead of the game, M.C. called me to come and pick up his suitcase a couple of days early so we could pack our trunk and be ready to go. The next morning, Hazel, M.C.'s wife, called us rather early. With a trembling voice she told me she had found M.C. sitting peacefully in his living room chair following his early morning run. He was dead of a massive heart attack at the relatively young age of 63.

Very few people are aware of the powerful influence M.C. Nelson exerted on the history of North Central. When the college was without a president, it was M.C. Nelson who managed the team, urged frugality, stocked the teaching pool with very capable adjunct faculty, and coordinated the recruitment of students from every nook and cranny. It was M.C. Nelson who paved the way for the incredible step of accreditation for our university. He led with the

Chapter Four

pride of the U.S. Army, taught with the passion and humor of an old friend, and wept with the weak and hurting because of his own acquaintance with the tragedies of life. M.C. officiated for our wedding, mentored me in my early ministry, coached me on my preaching, and loved me like a dad.

M.C. Nelson died some 30 years ago, yet his impact on North Central lives on. He and many others like him walked the halls of our institution, leaving a powerful mark while their personal stories have passed into the Ages. He is the representative of the fabric of North Central University in the 21st Century.

Mike Shields served as the Minnesota District Youth Director for many years, and then they served as missionaries to Chile. Presently Mike and Mona Shields are missionary evangelists to Latin America. Through their ministries, thousands have come to know Christ.

Surrendering Our Lives: North Central Memories 1971-1974

Philip D. McLeod

My most vivid memory of life at North Central was the Spiritual Emphasis week that took place in the fall of 1971, led by Dick Eastman. As a child, I grew up attending the Minneapolis Gospel Tabernacle and had significant connections to North Central Bible College. I began my college career at the University of Minnesota and transferred to North Central after I sensed God's call on my life for ministry.

The weekend before, Dick Eastman spoke at a youth retreat presented by the Minneapolis Gospel Tabernacle. I attended that retreat and was challenged to pray and seek God at a depth that I had not yet encountered in my life to that point. Following the retreat, my heart was prepared for God's work through the Spiritual Emphasis week.

A very unusual occurrence took place in one of the evening services. A strong sense of conviction came upon the service as Dick Eastman spoke about the things that were hindering us from a deeper walk with God. I do not recall exactly how it began, but students were leaving the chapel, returning with the objects and things that were keeping them from intimacy with God. As the students returned they were placing them on the altar.

This lasted for an extended period of time as I was able to drive to my home about ten minutes from campus and return with the items that I felt the Lord was asking me to lay down. A collection of things from stereos to sporting goods to you name it was at the altar.

As the years have unfolded, I have often returned in my mind to that night, and I realize that the specific item that I surrendered was not what mattered, but that act of surrender lives on and will continue to impact my future. In fact, as I have reminisced about that night and shared with friends, that night could never be duplicated because it was a one-time work of God in hearts that were tender and prepared for the Spirit's gentle touch to shape our lives.

That first Spiritual Emphasis week marked me for a lifetime in a powerful and dynamic way. Two distinct things were accomplished in my life that made my experience at NCBC more valuable than I could have imagined. The first was that it provided me a specific, personal spiritual encounter that validated my pursuit of God's call. Second, it confirmed to me the marked contrast between a state university educational experience and the life-changing experience that a Christian or Bible college could provide.

A second powerful memory I have of my years at NCBC was the significant influence of professors David Johnson and Wesley Smith. In very different ways, these men were used by God to integrate faith and learning in the academic experience at college. Both men saw potential and fostered it through daily challenges to me to think more critically about the Word and work of God.

Professor Smith was and is the best Bible teacher I have ever heard. He taught me to be a student of the Word. Professor Johnson helped me to relate my abilities to my future opportunities for ministry by his continuing encouragement to explore God's many pathways for service. There is no way to fairly and completely assess the impact these two men had on my life. I cherish them as friends to this very day.

Phil McLeod is the vice president for academic affairs at Valley Forge Christian College in Pennsylvania.

A Time of Definition

Rocky and Sherry Grams

A time of definition, a time of finding God faithful and real in our own lives, a time so packed with emotions and challenges that I can still sense the weariness of taking on so much simultaneously. But we found friendship and trust, connected with caring people, found ourselves and found each other!

Sherry and I met at North Central Bible College. That is cause enough to continually bless the school! We worked together on the school newspaper, *The Northern Light*, and worked side by side in the Latin American prayer band. We planned picnics and fund raising breakfasts as class officers and sang together in the Evangelaire Choir.

North Central was the place of meeting God, finding our vocation, and trying our wings. Some of our first teaching, preaching, planning and organizing were made possible by North Central's excellent mix of devotion, practics and teaching of the Word. Sherry worked in the cafeteria and then in the library. I worked as night guard at the school on weekends.

Classes with Brother Ray Levang were unforgettable, especially his jokes and essay tests over all of the material. Other faculty made an impact on us: Brother J.P. Phillipps' tender spirit and respect for the Word; Brother William Snow's love for the students and bemused flexibility when we presented some harebrained motion in our parliamentary procedure practices; Sister Ione Soltau's love of kids and positive view of us and of God's work; Wes Smith's friendship and challenges toward growth; the impacting move of God when Dick Eastman ministered to us. There are so many memories that have put down the base of trust in our hearts and minds and spirits.

The 435 people of the student body gave over $40,000 in one offering that week of Spiritual Impact toward the new chapel. I emptied out my savings – not a lot there – but the money paid for a few bricks anyway in that place of God's presence.

The backdrop of our experience at North Central has affected how we teach and administer God's dream here in Buenos Aires at Institute Biblico Rio de la Plata.

Yes, we bless North Central with our whole heart!

Rocky and Sherry Grams have served in Argentina as missionaries for over 25 years. Rocky is the Director of IBRP, the Assemblies of God Bible School in Buenos Aires, and they have helped to train most of the strong leaders in the famous Argentine revival.

A God Season

Pastor Max J. Meyers

It was March 1976, and I was a second semester freshman. My pregnant wife Nina had to quit her job in the IDS Tower because she

Chapter Four

had "morning sickness" in the morning, afternoon, and night. I worked afternoons as a teller at Marquette Bank, raking in a hair over minimum wage. The Veterans Administration had stopped my benefit checks for several months due to a clerical error. The rent on our little one-bedroom apartment had been due two weeks earlier. The building manager stopped by to collect money I didn't have. I'd never been behind on anything in my life. Food was running out.

"Surely, God will provide today," I thought. "Surely money will somehow appear in my mailbox." But no money was there. It was a notice from the North Central Bible College business office, telling me that if I didn't pay my tuition bill up to date that I would not be able to attend classes.

Passionate and deep theological discussions were frequently started by my wife. Most of them ended with, "It is obvious that you are out of the will of God. Surely you have made a gross error in thinking that God has called you to ministry. If you were in God's will, we would not have our world falling down around us."

Tears. Pain. Confusion. Disillusionment. No food. No money. No hope. I did something that I now know sounds bizarre. I beat my head against the hard plaster walls of our apartment. "God, where are you?"

I don't remember who initiated it, but within days of that question I sat in Dr. Argue's office. He said something to me that I will never forget. "Max, you are called into ministry. Don't quit school. We will work it out." Nina and I are eternally grateful to Dr. Argue. His affirmation kept us on God's course for our lives and brought us hope. This one event encapsulates what my season at NCBC was like. Full of challenges, met with affirmation and encouragement from both faculty and administration.

Every decade has political, social, and spiritual characteristics that make it unique. For the mid to late nineteen seventies, it was post-Vietnam, the Equal Rights Amendment, bus ministries, and the emergence of "televangelism." The post-war environment didn't seem to manifest itself on campus, but the other three did. In Bible class on the books of Timothy, professor Bob Bayless picked some individuals to debate the issue: "Should women have leadership roles in the church?" Out of the four students chosen for this debate, another brother and I were given the role of defending the position that women were not meant for leadership. (Oh, great.)

After a week to prepare our material, we were on stage, ready to debate the other position. It was at that moment that I got a taste of what a lawyer must feel like trying to defend a client that they know is guilty. It didn't take long for our position to sink like a rock. What made matters worse for me was that my partner was passionately convinced that our position was correct. He hollered and threw antagonistic volleys back at the other two. It all seems quite benign now, but at the time I felt like I would forever be looked upon as a narrow-minded chauvinistic, women-hater. Perhaps the fact that I vividly remember the embarrassment of the event indicates the need for therapy?

The other cultural winds blowing across the campus were the emergence of church growth through bus ministries and the emergence of Jim Bakker and Jimmy Swaggart on the national scene. It was all about building big ministries. The guest speakers for chapel were often the guys out there who had discovered the secret of how to grow a big church fast. Time and again we heard of their great successes with fleets of old school buses. Scrape some money together. Appoint bus captains. Have them spend all day Saturday knocking on doors. On Sunday, pick up your throng of children who can't wait to get inside your church. Then for the adults, your city will knock your doors down if you have "big events." Just book professional sports figures or celebrities, and before you know it you will be in your second or third building program.

For us pastors in training, it was a formula made in heaven!

Chapter Four

Suffice it to say that many of us went to our first pastorate, confident that we would instantly build the next mega-church. Why not? It was working for those other pastors. Well, it didn't work like that for most of us. What did work, though, was the cry of us young pastors at our altars early in the morning, desperately seeking God for His plan when our plans had failed.

Of course, I learned a lot of valuable information in the classroom of North Central over those years, but it was what happened outside of those rooms while I was a student that God used to shape me. As a United Methodist transplant, I was out of my element with these people called the "Assemblies of God." I was learning AG culture, systems, theology, and history. Over those four years, it became my culture, my systems, my theology, and my history. The United Methodists appointed me to pastor two churches near the Omaha area after graduation, but I couldn't accept the position. I was a different man than the one who entered NCBC four years previously.

Over the years, I have often heard my peers talk about their NCBC experiences. Dorm life stories and roommate encounters pepper their accounts. I can hardly ever relate. While they were experiencing campus community on an ongoing basis, it was a life that I would only pass through for hours in a day. When not on campus for my last three years as a full-time student, I worked a full-time job, volunteered on staff at a church, became a parent, and tried to hold together a marriage.

I began this account with speaking of my marriage, and that is how I want to tie this journey back together. Nina and I had a marriage that was caught in quicksand. We were constantly in conflict, and neither of us had the tools to know how to get us out of it. We were hopelessly sinking towards divorce. That is, until the administration brought to the campus a former pastor from Ohio who had started a new ministry called "Emerge." We were ready to receive from this man, Dr. Richard Dobbins. It was through those marriage seminars on campus that we received the tools we needed to turn our marriage around.

My season at NCBC was a God season that laid a foundation for the rest of my life. In perspective, I have to say that one of the greatest lessons I learned is that being a student of life is just as important as being a student in the classroom. Keep teaching me, Lord!

Presently Max Myers and his wife Nina are pastoring the Assemblies of God church in Hutchinson, Minnesota.

Chapter Five

Historical Review 1980-2005

Researched and written by
Jonathan Porter, North Central University student

Growth is the best word to describe the last 25 years from 1980-2005 – growth not just numerically, but academically and spiritually. The curriculum has expanded with the times, yet the same ministry focus is the heartbeat. Buildings have been added, and accreditation has been achieved. Student dress rules continue to shift. Just imagine this present generation wearing uniforms! But what has not changed is that same passion for the Lord evidenced in the students. Numerous and inspiring are the highlights of the last several decades at North Central.

Administrative Changes

Accreditation is a necessity for any reputable college, and North Central has made an effort to keep its standards high. In the early 1980's, North Central Bible College was accredited with the

American Association of Bible Colleges (AABC). In 1986 the college became regionally accredited with the Higher Learning Commission of the North Central Association (NCA) of Colleges and Schools.

After one of the comprehensive visits by an NCA Team in 1998, the Board of Regents voted to change the name of North Central Bible College to North Central University.

Assemblies of God districts in the upper Midwest own and operate North Central. In 1974, the districts included Minnesota, Iowa, South Dakota, Wisconsin/Upper Michigan, and Illinois. Over the next several years, the following districts voted to become part of North Central: North Dakota, Nebraska, Northern Missouri, Indiana, Michigan, and Midwest Latin American District. Over the years, committed members of the Board of Regents have made decisions which have helped the college to grow and maintain its strong ministry focus.

Majors

Present students may find it difficult to believe that, in 1980, North Central had bachelor of science and bachelor of arts degrees in only seven majors: Pastoral Studies, Missions Education, Christian Education, Sacred Music, Behavioral Sciences and Interdisciplinary Ministries. The 1980's brought a time of growth in the degree programs during which North Central added several majors.

Among these new majors was Youth Ministries, which is one of North Central's most popular majors. The Elementary Education program was also created during this time, a major that is known for its challenging yet rewarding program. The Church Planting and Communications majors were approved during the 1980's as well.

One area of ministry that makes North Central unique is the Deaf Culture major. Pioneered by church planter Carol Vetter along with Emory Dively, this program has affected outreach to one of the largest unreached people groups that exists. The Deaf Culture Ministries student learned how to preach and minister effectively

Chapter Five

within the Deaf community. Various Deaf were in pastoral studies programs, and an ASL/English Interpreter program was added for hearing students.

Because the college is in an urban area, it was natural that the University would add an Urban Ministries major designed for students who felt God calling them to minister in urban settings. An extra impetus for development came with the award of a Pew Charitable Trust Grant for about $750,000 in the late 1990's. The grant was directed by Dr. Paul Freitag with support from Dr. Carolyn Tennant.

At the end of the millennium, NCU added an English major and a Business major – a program last offered by the institution in 1945. As back then, this major was different from a public university's program in that it had a ministry focus. In 2005, an Accounting major was added.

The major, Teaching English as a Foreign Language (TEFL) was for students who desired to reach the world for Christ through language instruction. Students learned how to communicate the love of Christ across many cultures because of this major. The TEFL program was offered by the Intercultural Studies and Languages department, the missions training department of North Central. Its curriculum focuses upon world issues and themes of biblical justice to prepare effective communicators of the gospel in the new millennium. An Evangelism major was added, along with a Campus Ministries major designed to reach the university campuses where many students need to hear the salvation message of Christ.

In the new Fine Arts department, majors in Contemporary Christian Music, Music Performance, Theatre and Music Business were added to the academic repertoire. The most recent addition, Music Business, gave students the ability to be salt and light in that challenging industry.

The ever-growing Youth Ministries department added a Youth Development Studies major meant to appeal to those called to work with youth outside the church setting. Whether they wanted to be a soccer coach or a youth counselor, students learned how to reach the world of youth.

In the late 1990's major revamping of all curriculum resulted in the development of Supporting Programs. These allowed students to train in multiple areas of interest and calling. In line with the university vision to have both an urban and global focus, NCU also added numerous opportunities to connect to our society both at home and abroad. Various overseas programs were added to the curriculum including study abroad, missions trips for various departments, and overseas internships. For example, the Elementary Education department regularly sponsored an overseas student teaching experience, and the Business department developed business plans that assisted a town in a third world country. Faculty members and students traveled to the site for implementation. The Student Life department also sponsored student trips over spring break. Called "ninedays," these service-oriented trips allowed students to minister across the world in orphanages, urban centers, on Native American reservations, and in various missions projects.

The G. Raymond Carlson Institute for Church Leadership provided distance education courses and master's degree courses in conjunction with the Assemblies of God Theological School. Established in the 1980's by Dr. Gordon Anderson, the Carlson Institute has a long history of helping non-traditional students reach their educational dreams. To continue this effort, North Central established a degree completion program which will offer degree completion classes to non-traditional students in the fall of 2006.

North Central has been a school that has offered numerous opportunities to its students, and the school will continue to give everyone a chance to discover their ministry and hone their God-given talents.

Chapter Five

Student Organizations

North Central has always encouraged its students to grow and develop leadership abilities. Over the past 25 years there have been various student organizations, but they all have been about one thing, servant leadership.

S.T.E.A.M. was the name of student government in the 1980's, and it stood for "Students involved with Total Environment for Active Ministry." Though S.T.E.A.M. no longer exists under that name, it has evolved into the NCSA cabinet. The NCSA (North Central Student Association) was formed to serve the students. The leadership consists of a president, vice-president, and various directors. The several branches that stem from the NCSA include the following: Leadership Development Committee (created to further the servant leadership skills of NCU students), Student Activities Committee (organizes entertaining events for students), Student Relations Committee (communicates what is happening on campus), Student Ministry Board (provides ministry opportunities for students), and the Student Senate (officers that are elected to form relations with the NCU officials and bring beneficial change for the students)

Students during the 1980's had the opportunity to be a part of *The Archive* which was the school's yearbook. Each volume provided a pictorial remembrance of college life at North Central. The last issue was published in 1993. A particular organization that has stood the test of time is the student newspaper *The Northern Light*. For years *The Northern Light* has informed students, providing campus, local and national news.

North Central has always had a large number of married students. In the 1980's, nearly one-fourth of the students were married, and in the 1990's approximately one-fifth. The name of their student organization changed throughout the years from the Married Students Fellowship to the Marriage Connection and then

A Faithful Past, A Shining Future

One In Heart. The goal of this organization was to provide fellowship and support among the married students.

Missionary kids have attended the school since the beginning of North Central's history. Mu Kappa North was formed in the late 1980's as a fellowship to meet the unique needs of MKs.

Students across the decades have participated in class organizations. Every year the student body elected officers to represent each class (freshman through senior). Whoever was elected would conduct business meetings during class chapels and plan various events on campus. Each group would plan get-togethers that would edify their class. Some of the events included the Fall Fest Days, "Sadie Hawkins," and the Spring Banquet.

Students Communicating Christ to All Nations (SCCAN) was a student organization that worked hard to raise funds for missions, plan and implement the annual Missions Emphasis, publish monthly flyers, and review student applicants planning on doing missions overseas. SCCAN brought global awareness to North Central so that they would be in tune with what was happening around the world.

Throughout the years there have always been numerous excellent musical groups established at North Central. Many students of the past will remember the original look, feel, and sound of One Accord when it was established by Larry Bach in 1984. While the look and style may have changed, the goal of One Accord has not. They have always desired to share God's love through song and praise.

Numerous other organizations of different types were started during the 1980's. These included Brother and Sister Floor activities with the Resident Advisors and a new program of small groups called the Caring Connection. A mentoring program was also instituted. The R.A.s held retreats at the beginning of the year, usually going camping. Other training was established including the first leadership class which enrolled 100 in the course. Between 200-300 students were involved in student leadership each year. Leadership

Chapter Five

opportunities have continued to expand, and a Leadership minor was added to the curriculum in 2004. North Central has gained a national reputation for training Christ-like servant leaders.

The Rules Have Changed

If a 21st century North Central student were to walk into the college 20 years ago, they would be in for a shock. Likewise, if a student from the early 1980's were to wander into Phillipps Hall today and find a television or into a classroom and see women in jeans, they might indeed be flabbergasted.

North Central has always encouraged good judgment among students as to how a Christian should dress. However in the 1980's, the school had a different dress code. Women were required to wear dresses or skirt and blouse outfits for class and chapel. Nowadays women may wear jeans, shorts, and T-shirts during academic hours, but they are still asked to dress modestly.

In the 1980's men wore dress shirts and dress slacks for class and chapel. As a matter of fact, most of the men chose to dress up even more. Suits and sports jackets were not uncommon in the hallways. Thankfully, students were allowed to wear blue jeans after main school hours at 4 p.m. It might be difficult trying to play football in dress slacks! The men were to be clean-shaven at all times. Beards were not an option until Gordon Anderson became president in 1995.

As the years went by, North Central administrators decided to update the dress code. The fall of 1992 was the first time women could have a choice of whether to wear dress slacks or skirts to class. By 1998 the school decided to become less specific with their dress code. Students have the responsibility to use spiritual discernment in this area.

In the early days, the movie theatre, as well as all forms of media, were either greatly discouraged or against the rules. In the early

1980's students were expected to steer clear from various forms of entertainment such as movies and dancing. By the late 1980's, with media access a public norm, students were allowed to have television sets in the dormitories and apartments. DVD and VCR players were not allowed until the fall of 2004. Today at NCU, students have more "freedom," but are still expected to act with Christ-like integrity.

Some rules will always be in place due to the damaging nature of participating in certain activities. Students will always be asked to abstain from alcohol, tobacco use, drugs, fornication, and gambling. Though society is shifting, students are taught how to live holy lives and to make choices throughout their day that are based upon their Christian beliefs.

Urban Context

The Twin Cities continued to provide a challenging setting for NCBC. Students were able to use the many resources that the cities provide. Minneapolis is like a learning lab for every class, and professors often incorporate assignments which will get students in the real world around them. It also offers concerts, theater, sports, various activities and shopping.

The numerous Assemblies of God churches in the Twin Cities area assimilate our students into a wide variety of ministries. North Central students teach children, work with youth, participate with worship teams, and serve in many different areas of church work. As a matter of fact, students must successfully complete at least four semesters of service before they can graduate. Students also serve in our community ministering on the streets and working with various service agencies.

The University lived out its "urban and international emphasis" by offering opportunities like tutoring immigrants in the local Somalian Ubah School, led by Dr. Buzz Brookman, and the music education program known as WOVEN (With One Voice Energizing

Chapter Five

Neighborhoods), directed by Joanne Kersten with support by Dianne Anderson and Beth Ann Rockett. The Student Life department also directed numerous urban outreach opportunities such as the annual Community Outreach Day, the Halloween neighborhood ministry, and local youth athletic events. Many students volunteered or worked at the Augustana nursing home, Elliot Park, the Hennepin County Medical Center, or with the homeless and needy.

Minneapolis has provided a bountiful supply of jobs over the decades, and the lucrative job market is still available today. Students of each decade have been able to take advantage of getting jobs that are a walk or bus ride away. In 2004, students had the option of riding the new light rail train system to access other jobs, like those at the Mall of America, the largest shopping complex in the United States. The students are able to get practical experience as well as develop leadership skills.

President Don Argue

Leadership is a word that every student who has spent his or her college years at North Central knows. "Servant leadership" is a phrase that every student has seen from the top down. From the president to the resident advisor, the heart of a servant is predominant. North Central has been blessed with amazing presidents.

In May 1979, Dr. Don Argue became the president of North Central Bible College. During his presidency, North Central grew both numerically and spiritually. Expansion was the main concern during Argue's 16 years of service. Not only was North Central the fastest growing private college in Minnesota, it was also one of the fastest growing colleges in the U.S. Enrollment was 401 in 1975 and grew to 1182 during the next decade. In recognition of this, North Central was given the decade of growth award from *Christianity Today* magazine.

A Faithful Past, A Shining Future

There were many challenges during Dr. Argue's presidency. One of the biggest was adding new facilities for the growing student population. As usual, God proved Himself faithful time and time again.

While the enrollment was growing and the property of North Central was expanding, President Argue still kept a humble heart for God, his faculty, staff and students. He did not just look at the material. Argue took joy in the way the Lord blessed the students with spiritual growth and maturity. Many knew Argue as someone who was "believable, knowledgeable, and helpful."

President Argue was brought up in a Pentecostal environment. He was raised in a pastor's home and was saved at a young age. When Argue was in high school he felt the Lord calling him to a deeper relationship. In his sophomore year Don fully committed himself to the Lord and received a call to ministry. Argue's renewed passion for God allowed him to be more sensitive to the Holy Spirit. Little did this teenager know that God was going to take him to places he never would have imagined.

In May 1961 Argue graduated from Central Bible College. Argue received his diploma, but he still had no idea where the Lord was taking him. All he knew was that he had several weeks of preaching ministry ahead of him with the Crusader's Trio. Though he had no detailed plans, he did have a servant's heart and love for others.

The doors began to open after he finished preaching with the Crusaders. Argue was offered the position of Director of Evangelism for Teen Challenge in New York City. Argue's new ministry opportunity paid him $10 a week, along with food and housing. Dr. Argue and his wife, Pat, had to pinch every penny to get by.

Eventually the Lord led Argue to San Jose, California, to be a youth pastor. Later he became the pastor of First Assembly of God, Morgan Hills, California. Then he accepted the position of dean of students and campus pastor at Evangel College.

Chapter Five

"Until the world is reached and the Lord returns, we are not through," President Argue said in an interview over 20 years ago. "I simply want to be in the place where I can be the most effective for the Kingdom." In 1974 Dr. Argue joined the North Central family, and in May 1979 he became president of NCBC. This president showed the student body as well as those around him that he wanted to be in a place where God could use him in the most effective way for the kingdom.

After 16 years of ministering to the students, faculty, and staff of North Central, Argue believed God was leading him to the next step of his ministerial calling. Dr. Argue left the college in May 1995 to serve as president of the National Association of Evangelicals (NAE). In 1999 he accepted the presidency of Northwest University in Kirkland, Washington.

Over 20 years ago, Don Argue said that his personal goals were to have total transparency and complete dependence upon God, and to work for his glory. He never dreamt of becoming the president of anything, he said, yet he has been the president of three separate institutions. A long time ago a teenager decided to be an instrument that God could use in any way. Perhaps this is why he became who he was to the students at North Central – a man who let God use him in extraordinary ways.

Vice President Don Meyer

The other Don of this period was Dr. Don Meyer. He served at North Central for 21 years, 18 of those as the Vice President of Academic Affairs.

Meyer was raised on a dairy farm in Lebanon, Pennsylvania. His original plan was to follow in his father's footsteps and go into farming. When he was a junior in high school, his father passed away, and God used this unfortunate event to show Meyer his call to ministry.

After graduation Meyer worked on the farm in order to save money for college. At the time Meyer was struggling with whether he should even go on to school due to the advice of some family friends. They believed he should just stay on the farm "because the second coming was so near." To them, school was just a waste of time. But then his father's cousin, Nathan Meyer, gave him some advice he would never forget. He told young Meyer, "The time you take to sharpen your tools is never wasted."

With confidence Meyer packed his bags and made his way to Central Bible College in the fall of 1964. Meyer will never forget his days at CBC, specifically because that is where he met his wife, Evie.

Shortly after graduation, Meyer and his bride moved to northwestern Pennsylvania to become a pastor in a local church where he served for seven years. Although Meyer loved pastoring, he sensed that God was calling him to become a professor. Eventually the Lord led Meyer and his family from the church in Franklin, Pennsylvania to Wheaton Graduate School in Wheaton, Illinois where he earned an M.A.T.S. degree.

Meyer began to apply at several AG colleges to teach, and North Central was on that list. In the fall of 1976 Meyer began his career teaching Old Testament, Church History, Bible Geography, and Greek.

Meyer loved teaching at North Central. It was a dream that God had planted in his heart, and he was more than happy to fulfill it. But during his third year of teaching God began to give him a desire for administrative ministry. What Meyer did not know was that President Clark was to resign that year, and Dr. Argue was to be the new president. To Meyer's surprise, Argue asked him to be the Academic Dean. Even after Meyer became Vice President, he continued to teach a Pentateuch class required for every incoming student. It was taught at 7 a.m. three days a week, and many a student from that period remembers Dr. Meyer's wisdom and wit, including his famous note cards.

Chapter Five

While Don Meyer left North Central in 1997, he said he will always remember the outstanding faculty, hard-working staff, loyal administrators, and the amazing student body. In his words Don Meyer said that "North Central was more than a place to work, it was for us a way of life."

After leaving NCU Dr. Don Meyer became president of Valley Forge Christian College in Pennsylvania which has seen much enrollment growth and change on the campus.

Dr. Gordon Anderson

Born November 11, 1946 in Scottsbluff, Nebraska, Dr. Gordon Anderson attended the University of Colorado and then in 1970 received a bachelor's degree in religion from Southern California College. He was ordained by the Assemblies of God in 1973 while serving as senior pastor at Chapel of the Plains Assembly of God in Stoneham, Colorado. From 1974 to 1982, Anderson pastored the Life Center Assembly of God in Portland, Oregon. During this time he earned a bachelor's degree in philosophy and a master's degree in history from the University of Portland.

In 1982 Gordon Anderson moved to Minneapolis with his wife Dianne and his two boys to serve as a professor at North Central Bible College. Anderson earned his Ph.D. in ancient studies in 1986 at the University of Minnesota. His diverse experiences at NCU include pastoral leadership, professor and chair of the department of Liberal Arts. He was also the founder and director of the G. Raymond Carlson Institute for Church Leadership at North Central from 1989 to 1993.

In 1993 Dr. Anderson and his wife Dianne served in the mission field as director of the Eurasia Office for the Assemblies of God Division of World Missions. He became the sixth president of NCU in May 1995 and was honored by the Board of Regents in the fall of 2005 for serving with great effectiveness over a decade.

A Faithful Past, A Shining Future

In addition to his duties at North Central, Anderson serves as a General Presbyter for the Assemblies of God and was a member of the National Commission for Doctrinal Purity. In 1997, Anderson chaired the Spiritual Life Committee for the General Council. Dr. Anderson's broad experience as a pastor, missionary and student of revivals prepared him to lead the university into the new millennium.

The chapel was always full when Anderson preached each Friday, followed by a time of prayer and fasting. Dr. Anderson understood and believed in the present generation of students. It always brought a smile to students' faces when he reminded them that they were "clearly superior."

North Central Expands

The greater portion of the last decade was dedicated to providing the students and faculty with necessary facilities.

One of the first expansions made in the 1980's was the building of the Clark Danielson College Life Center (CLC). While the need for this building was dire, the college faced many challenges in laying the foundation for its new building. North Central received many pledges of financial support. Unfortunately, due to a nation-wide economic hardship of the 1970's, many of the original donors could not pay their pledges.

When the College Life Center was near completion, the school was completely out of funds to finish construction. God, however, was in control. No one lost heart because they knew that the Lord was in the whole situation. At a chapel service, President Argue told students and faculty to begin praising God for their brand new facility, even though it had not yet been completed. As one united body, North Central believed together that God was going to fulfill his promise.

By God's provision the building was completed in the spring of 1981. Students and faculty were more than happy with their new

Chapter Five

chapel and the College Life Center whose facilities included a brand new gymnasium, administrative offices, and five classrooms on the second floor. During the bitter Minnesota winter months, students remained warm and toasty as they walked across the skyways, free from the snow and blistering winds. Skyways connecting the Chapel to Miller Hall, and the CLC to Carlson Hall were completed in the spring of 1981.

Due to the rapid increase in student population, as well as the large number of married and non-traditional students, North Central purchased the five Orfield apartment buildings behind Miller Hall in the winter of 1981. Both affordable and close, students still live there today. A large home adjacent to the campus was purchased and refurbished as the T.J. Zimmerman House, an honors house for male students.

Classes continued to grow, and the college needed even more classrooms. North Central purchased the one-story building located behind the chapel building and moved the Communications department there in 1988. In 1989 North Central obtained Elliot East, refurbished storefronts that became the home of the Deaf International Bible College, Carlson Institute, Cross Cultural Ministries, the Behavioral Science department, and a number of classrooms. In 1998, the buildings were named the Del Kingsriter Centre. American Legion Hall across the street from the Kingsriter Centre was purchased and transformed into classroom space known as Centennial Hall. Also during this time North Central purchased controlling interest in the Elliot East condominiums.

In 1994 the college acquired the Trestman property on the southwest area of Chicago Avenue and 14th Street. Alumni and faculty remember that Giswold's Drugstore, affectionately known as "Gizzies" by the students, was located there. The current Chicago Hall was originally Little Judge's, a liquor store. Ironically, when North Central purchased the property in 1994, the liquor store had to remain open until the owner's lease expired. After the expiration, the store was closed and the building was fully renovated and was first used by the Fine Arts department for music practice rooms.

In the summer of 2004, Chicago Hall went through another facelift. The Youth Ministries department was growing and in need of their own facilities. By the fall the Center for Youth and Leadership had a home. Along with new classrooms and meeting rooms, the Center is home to the Basement coffee shop and youth resources library.

The Phillipps Hall project was North Central's largest construction plan to date. It was not just a building that needed renovation; it was a dream built from scratch. The original building concept was a 10-story dormitory with a new cafeteria. The projected price tag of $11 million forced college officials to rethink their plans. An alternate, two-phase plan was created. The building was redesigned into a four-story, 64,000 square foot residence hall without a cafeteria.

In the fall of 2000, Phase I of the "Building Upon the Legacy" development program was complete with the dedication of the building. Its namesake is Dr. John Phillipps, a dedicated alumnus, faculty member and administrator who taught at North Central from 1949 to 1981. Phillipps Hall became home to 240 students while its lower level contained North Central's main computer classroom.

Phase II of the project was the renovation of the cafeteria. The cafeteria facilities were in dire need of change. The restoration process completed a new cafeteria, kitchen, student union and deli. By September of 2001, the renovations were complete. The new cafeteria included self-serve bars for stir-fry, deli meat, main entree, soups, and salads. The spacious, well-lit dining hall was a welcome addition.

In the summer of 2004, a 35,000 square foot building known as the Beth Mensing Memorial Kidney Center was donated to the campus. Located near the Hennepin Country Medical Center, Mensing Hall was once linked to the hospital as housing for long-term patient care. The building was renovated in 2004 to include student housing and new facilities for the Fine Arts department: practice rooms, faculty offices, music lab, classrooms, and sound studios. Crews constructed a professional-quality recording studio in one wing of the building, which will be used by students to study recording arts and music production.

Most recently, North Central remodeled the F.J. Lindquist chapel, added a 200-seat auditorium, and built a new two story atrium. The resulting complex has been renamed as the new Thomas E. Trask Word and Worship Center. The vision for the new building is that it will serve as the center of worship for the campus, by offering an excellent venue for worship and performance, and for the instruction of communicating the "Word" – homiletics training.

The Spiritual Life of North Central

The spiritual life of North Central centered on the chapel service experience. Many alumni remember the powerful moments spent at the altar or when a certain guest speaker was speaking directly to them. For some it was when they were used in the gifts of the Spirit for the first time, and for others it was when God showed them their calling. Without the Spirit of God North Central was nothing more than an institution. Thankfully, the University emphasized the importance of having a fruitful walk with God. Students and faculty daily saw the power of God, in and out of the classroom. There were regular testimonies shared of healings and God's provision, of family members and work associates getting saved and being thoroughly changed.

Every Friday after chapel there was time of fasting and prayer. Dr. Don Argue and Don Meyer testified that one of the reasons for the college's growth during the 1980's was due to the quality of the chapel services. That quality and vision continues to this day. There is a bond that happens in chapel that can only happen through the Holy Spirit.

Due to the crowded atmosphere of the chapel, officials decided to add a second, student-led chapel which started in 2000. This chapel was designed for students in church ministries to practice their preaching, worship leading, and altar ministry.

North Central has carried a long tradition of having a Spiritual Emphasis week. Earlier students will remember the young curly haired youth speaker Rich Wilkerson who came on more than one occasion (1981 and 1984). Still others will remember speakers such as the passionate Reverend Jack Hayford (1983) or the challenging John Palmer (1987). These speakers, among others, spoke into the lives of both students and faculty.

Also during this time monthly all night prayer meetings became highlights for many. Students would pray for their nation and the school, as well as for personal needs. This brought North Central closer to the Lord and each other.

While students loved going to chapel to hear speakers and pray, they also wanted a time when they could worship without being limited to a set time. In 1984, Dr. Carolyn Tennant, who was Vice President for Student Life at the time, thought of a way where students could have that opportunity. She believed that the best time for this to occur would be on Wednesday nights after church, and she was right. This was a place where students gathered together and praised the Lord, hence the name, Praise Gathering. After a night of ministering to others, students gathered together to pray, worship and rejuvenate. The Holy Spirit came with full force as students yearned for a real touch from God. Healings and prophetic words were common blessings during this time. For almost 21 years, North Central Students attended and ran Praise Gathering on Wednesdays.

Chapter Five
Administration and Faculty

Many administration, faculty and staff have poured their lives into North Central. So many could be named and highlighted for their contributions. The following list is of current faculty and administration who have given over a decade of service to the university.

James Allen (1981): Professor of Practical Ministry, Campus Pastor, Chair of Pastoral department

Gordon Anderson: (1982) Professor and chair of General Education; Director of the Carlson Institute; President

Jerilyn Bach (1987): Assistant Professor of Education

Larry Bach (1981): Associate Professor of Music; Executive Director of Fine Arts

Cheryl Book (1983): Director of Admissions, Vice President of Business and Finance

Buzz Brookman (1978): Professor of Biblical Studies; Chair of Intercultural Studies and Languages

Leslie Crabtree (1981-93, 1998): Professor of English

Paul Freitag (1987): Student Life; Director of City Gate; Executive Assistant to the President for Resource Development

Ronald Jewett (1989): Professor of Psychology; Registrar

Joanne Kersten (1974-83, 1997): Associate Professor of Music

Margo Lloyd (1988): Professor of Elementary Education and Chair of Education department

Glen Menzies (1982): Student Life; Chair of Pastoral Ministries department; Professor of New Testament, Patristics

Dan Nelson (1989): Chair of Psychology department, Professor of Psychology, Assessment Coordinator

Mike Nosser (1996): Director of Retention; Vice President of Student Life

Dave Pedde (1992): Assistant Professor of Music

Dan Rector (1990): Assistant Professor of Children's Ministries

JoAnn Smith (1986): Associate Professor of Deaf Culture Studies; Director of the G. Raymond Carlson Institute for Church Leadership

Roger Sorbo (1982): Chair of Arts and Sciences, Professor

Carolyn Tennant (1983): Vice President of Student Life, Vice President of Academic Affairs, and Professor of English

Long term staff include Diane Canfield, Lee Holmer, Donna Jaeger, Joy Jewett, Linda Kammerer, Vern Kissner, Steve Krahn, Marvin Langmade, and Betty Smith.

Chapter Six

Alumni Stories 1980-2005

Fingerprints In a Foam Pillow

Pastor Mike Haseltine

North Central Bible College was my second college experience. I had attended another "Christian college" for two years before coming to North Central. I remember feeling a little depressed upon my first few weeks at NCBC because I felt "there was no one to witness to." I was always trying to lead someone to Christ at the other college, but here I was surrounded by students who beamed with a relationship with Jesus.

There are many things that are forever carved into my life from my experiences at NCBC. The vision casting of our President Don Argue, prayer meetings on the fifth floor dorm where I lived, study times in the library, theological discussions that would last late into the night, the small crowded cafeteria, the dished stairs worn over time under the feet of many eager students.

The two biggest, inescapable memories I have are of chapel and the faculty. I remember wondering why they even had to take chapel attendance. Why would anyone miss chapel?

Chapel was evidence of the very real, life-giving, and joy-radiating presence of the Holy Spirit. Words of prophecy, tongues and interpretation were the norm. As a young man with the call to preach on his life, I admired, listened intently to, and desperately hoped for God to use me like He was using these speakers.

The faculty were sacrificial servants of God. I felt the impact of their lives at the time. It was like the hand print in a foam pillow, except their hand prints have not disappeared; they have only become deeper as time has passed. Professor Snow said, "Now get to it," referring to preparing to preach, and "Prepare a meal people would want to eat" and "If you preach past noon, I don't care how anointed you think you are, you're preaching to the wall." These words have encouraged me to be done speaking before people were done listening.

Professor John Phillipps awakened a hunger for knowledge. I admired the years of his study and all his brain had retained. I was challenged to think, to reason through issues biblically. He caused me to want to be filled with the Spirit, using the gifts and developing the fruit without being a nut!

Academic Dean Don Meyer radiated life and joy, even as he taught Pentateuch at 7 a.m.! Brother Ian Hall, Bill Crew, David Owen, Missionaries in Residence Ken Krake and Jim Roane – names and lives with their fingerprints all over my life. I am filled with gratitude.

Pastor Michael Haseltine is a 1981 graduate of North Central. He is presently the Senior Pastor of Maranatha Assembly of God in Forest Lake, Minnesota.

Chapter Six
It's Time to Walk with God
Memories of Pastor Darrell Geddes
interview by Bethany Moeller, North Central University student

Darrell Geddes graduated from North Central in 1981. During his years in Bible college, he earned a degree in Pastoral Studies and also sang in the Chorale.

Some of Geddes' favorite professors were Ian Hall and John Phillipps. "They were excellent teachers, with a great grasp of the Word," says Pastor Geddes. He remembers John Phillips' New Testament class, attended by around 100 people and held in what was then the largest classroom, which is now the Elementary Education lab. Geddes describes Ian Hall's Pentecostal Distinctives class as the most pivotal course he took at North Central. "I was a Pentecostal, but I didn't really know why I was Pentecostal." By learning history and discussing issues, the class helped Geddes better understand why he believed what he did.

Another important lesson Geddes learned at North Central that has helped his ministry was a piece of advice that Professor Snow gave in a pastoral class. Snow taught them the importance of learning to "throw a velvet-colored brick." His challenge was to give constructive criticism with a cushion so that it would help people, not hurt them.

Geddes once reached a point when he was ready to drop out of North Central. During this time, President Argue preached a message in chapel entitled "It's Time to Walk with God." He spoke about Enoch's close relationship with God and challenged students like Geddes who felt like they might not be getting what they expected in their experience at North Central. The message was a profound one for Geddes. God got his attention at just the right time.

Upon graduation, Geddes went on to minister in Chicago in an inner city church. Afterward, he came to North Central as the first professor for the new Urban Ministries major. He was a prime mover in developing this program and also developed and tested much of the curriculum that was designed as part of a large grant to North Central through Pew Charitable Trusts. Today, he is the senior pastor of Christ Church International, the former Gospel Tabernacle where the University first started under Frank Lindquist in 1930.

Provisions

Tim Buttrey

If I've said it once, I've said it a thousand times. I love my alma mater, NCU! I don't think I expected my education or my experience there to be perfect. We've all heard the statement by preachers and evangelists: "Let me tell you something you won't learn in Bible college!" Nevertheless, my experience at NCU remains one of the most wonderful and influential seasons of my life.

After several years of rebellious running from my call to ministry I finally came to my senses in 1979 and ran back to God. Within months God had given me back the love of my heart, Linda, and we planned to marry and prepare for ministry together. I remember returning from a trip to check out one of our other AG colleges. I was very discouraged that it wasn't the place for me, and I prayed all the way home that God would give me direction. That very Sunday Dr. Don Argue was the guest speaker at my home church in Dayton, Ohio. The minute I talked to him he saw right through me, and he knew I was supposed to go to North Central. Instantly I, too, knew the same thing. I was a typical midwestern child of the 1970's with long hair and a gold cross earring – which had changed from the thunderbolt I had prior to my conversion! In Dr. Argue's smooth

Chapter Six

Canadian manner he assured me I would be a perfect fit at NCBC, but my earring and some of my hair would have to go.

A few months later I married my childhood sweetheart, Linda, and days later we packed up our bright yellow Gremlin to leave for NCBC. The worst part of that story is that I sold my 1971 British racing green Stingray Corvette to buy that humble little Gremlin. The day we were leaving we were all set to go except for the money we needed for fuel to get to Minneapolis. We prayed and checked the mailbox one last time. There was a check from my bank for the exact amount of money we needed for the trip. To this day we don't know why the bank sent us that check. We had closed the account weeks before!

God's miraculous provision happened many, many times over the next four years as students. Several really stand out among the rest. Once, shortly after our firstborn son Josh was born, we were completely out of food. We prayed like always. Within hours our apartment intercom alerted us to a visitor in the lobby. No one answered us on the intercom. Upon going down to the lobby we found several grocery bags filled with food!

Another time we were completely broke. I remember Linda and me sitting at our kitchen table that Saturday morning praying for a financial miracle. We decided to go out and enjoy that warm summer day down by the lakes. After returning home, there was a knock at our apartment door. Outside were two suspicious looking gentlemen wearing dark sunglasses and wreaking of cigarette smoke. They asked me if they could come in. I said, "No way."

They proceeded to show me their Minneapolis Police department badges and explained that they were detectives investigating suspicious activity at the manufacturing plant across the street from our apartment. They wanted to set up a tripod and camera somewhere in our building to take undercover pictures. They said they would give me $100 per week to use a window looking over the building in question with a guarantee of $500. They laid two crisp $100 bills on the kitchen table that Linda and I had just prayed for only hours earlier!

Although I had grown up in a Christian home, NCBC was the place where I learned virtually everything there was to know about being a disciple of Jesus Christ. I loved my classes with the likes of great teachers such as John Phillipps, Don Meyer, Gordon Anderson, Dave Mellberg, and Ernie Freeman. Doug Lowenberg always served as a mentor and role model. For years following graduation I found myself asking the question, "What would Doug Lowenberg do?" His integrity, wisdom, and convictions inspired me.

I flourished under the guidance of great leaders who modeled spiritual disciplines like fasting, praying, worshiping and studying. Chapels were always spectacular; I looked forward to every one of them. Without fail the presence of God was always affecting and changing lives. Whether it was a normal chapel, a special emphasis, or a morning where the Holy Spirit chose to invade our lives as we lingered around the altar, I tried never to miss. What I learned about the anointing and homiletics by listening to the great preachers and teachers who graced the chapel pulpit impacted the entirety of my ministry.

Perhaps one of the most significant events of my life happened when Doug Lowenberg and Glen Menzies presented my name to the leadership of the school for consideration as the Resident Dean of Men. I knew immediately that God had prepared me for that ministry. I prayed desperately to be given this opportunity. Serving as the Resident Dean during my senior year and ultimately becoming the Dean of Men for nearly four academic years was a highlight of my entire ministry. Working alongside of Carolyn Tennant, then Vice President for Student Life, and Debbie Jonnes, Dean of Women – not to mention all of the wonderful young men and women who served as Resident Advisors – was a real delight.

Chapter Six

I was blessed and honored to have Carolyn Tennant as my first "boss." She brought out the best in me and had a gift to cultivate and extract even more than you knew was in your heart. Most of the time I think it was her wisdom and creativity that prevailed, but she would end up giving me or others the credit. My wife Linda remembers many times that I'd come home to our modest little apartment in the dorm and say, "I love my job." She gave me so much confidence to attain my dreams that when I launched out on my own and went "west," I was saddened to realize that few places are like NCBC and few leaders are like Dr. Tennant. She deeply and permanently affected my leadership, priorities, and faith. I have more stories from those years as the Dean of Men than time or space allows – stories about the many wonderful students, late nights in the residence halls, Welcome Weeks, and R.A. training retreats.

Taking everything into consideration, relationships that were made and kept still remain my most valuable commodity throughout the years. Whether it is in my marriage to the love of my life, those I have led or pastored, the friends that I have made around the world, or my utter dependence on Jesus Christ, nothing in life is more important than being in right relationship. Thank you, NCU, for putting some of the most godly, inspiring people in the world into my life whose relationships with me affect every level of my life to this very day!

Tim Buttrey was the director of the Married Student Fellowship at NCBC from 1980 to 1983. He became the Resident Dean of Men and then the Dean of Men. Linda served on staff in the Accounting department. After serving at NCBC until 1986, Tim became the Young Adult Ministries Pastor in Covina, California and then for 10 years was the founding pastor of Crossroads Church in Temecula, California while Linda led their school. Today he is president of Restoration Resources Ministry and travels throughout the U.S. with his wife Linda conducting marriage seminars and other ministry.

Go to That Interview!

Loralie Crabtree

My first memories of North Central Bible College were as a young teen visiting the campus with my dad who was enrolled as a student. I could tell there was something special about the environment. It wasn't just the friendly faces and the intrigue of the old buildings in the middle of the big city. A distinct sense of God's presence permeated the hallways, sparkled in the eyes of the students, and captured my attention. Upon graduation from high school my parents encouraged me to check out other schools to make a well informed choice, but my decision to attend NCBC was already made at the ripe old age of 14.

My years as a student at NCBC were ones of exponential growth and accelerated discipleship! Every aspect of my experience propelled me closer to Jesus, including the biblical instruction in the classroom, the Spirit-filled worship and preaching in chapel, and social experiences with classmates in the dorms and in ministry endeavors.

Those who had the most profound impact on my life were the teachers who not only taught their subjects with expertise and clarity but also taught by their example what Christian leaders look and act like. Over the last nineteen years since my graduation from NCBC, I can see how choices I've made were influenced by professors who left their imprint on my faith and Christian character. Ernie Freeman taught me to think for myself and not merely be spoon-fed my beliefs. He taught me to examine the scriptures carefully to arrive at sound biblical conclusions. Bill Crew cared about me personally, asking after class if everything was okay when he noticed my grades slipping. He also made a surprise visit to the Friday night Elliot Park coffeehouse I directed and took time to affirm me and other students involved. Don Meyer taught me integrity and that "cream always rises to the top." He also taught me to be prepared for life's pop quizzes (remember those 3x5 cards?), and he impressed upon me the importance of encouraging others. I still have notes in my memory box that he wrote after I sang or led worship in chapel. Brother David Owen taught me to "give hilariously."

James Allen believed in me so much that he singled me out after class one day to encourage me to interview with a guest pastor for a youth pastor position. I didn't even think this pastor would consider me because of my gender, so I shied away from the opportunity. Dr. Allen would not let me hide behind my insecurities. I went to the interview and was hired. Dr. Allen's encouragement and affirmation launched me into nineteen wonderful years of ministry. I don't know what direction my life would have taken without Dr. Allen's gentle push. I appreciate his investment in my life more than he'll ever know!

Dr. Debbie Menken Gill showed me what a smart, spirit-filled woman looks like. She and Dr. Carolyn Tennant were two of the first women ministers I had ever encountered. I'm grateful for the example of both of these fine women. I hope there will always be women like them at NCU for other young women ministers to esteem and follow. I recall Dr. Tennant consoling me in the stairwell of Miller Hall after my boyfriend and I broke up. I still remember her gentle words of advice, and my husband (whom I met after graduation) appreciated her influence in my life as well!

I could go on and on about all the teachers: Dr. Phillipps, Gordon Anderson, Larry Goodrich, Larry Bach, Sandi Lowenberg Bradford, Jerry Falley. I could write endlessly about the way each of them has left their mark on my life and ministry.

Anyone who has attended North Central can never forget the amazing chapel services. Our worship in chapel became, in my mind, the standard by which all worship services should be measured. The worship was so authentic and uninhibited. It was so amazing to me to worship with such fervor with other people my age who shared the same passion for Jesus. The variety of chapel speakers challenged me in my Christian experience as well. Some who stand out in my mind are Jeanne Mayo as she preached on the all-consuming fire of God and literally, yet unintentionally, started the brand-new chapel carpet on fire with her illustrated sermon! Elizabeth Elliot and Jack Hayford challenged us to live lives of moral purity. Gordon Fee taught for a week on the Kingdom of God, exposing religiosity in my life and revealing Christ for who He really is. I cannot remember the names of many speakers, but I recall that my little world became very large as I listened to ministers literally from all over the world and from many walks of life.

And who can reminisce about North Central without recalling dorm life? I made some of the best friends of my entire life at NCBC. I'll never forget walking off the elevator on third floor the day I arrived on campus. I remember that the walls were painted blue, and the hall seemed so long. I nervously approached my assigned room and turned the handle to discover it was locked. A voice on the other side said, "Wait! I just got out of the shower!" I lingered a few minutes until a bath-robed sophomore with a towel on her head opened the door. Sue (Tomlin) Goodman became not only my roommate, but a dear friend, one with whom I still correspond and love to see at General Council. My circle of friends grew so large that I'm afraid if I began to make a list, I would omit some special person. But suffice it to say that the young men and women with whom I interacted each left their imprint on my life as well. I have a heart full of memories!

I could have chosen a different path. My grandmother offered to pay my entire way through school if I would attend the college of her choice. Although grandma's offer was enticing, I'm still glad I chose North Central Bible College. It effectively prepared me and launched

Chapter Six

me into a life of meaningful Pentecostal ministry. I trust that North Central will not only maintain but purposefully nurture its Spirit-filled environment so that generations to come can be shaped into lifelong Pentecostal leaders and learners.

Rev. Loralie (Robinson) Crabtree was an NCBC student from 1982 to 1986. She was involved in Chorale, served as the Elliot Park Ministries Director, was an on Evangelism Team with Ian Hall, served on the Hmong Outreach Team with Jerry Falley, and was on the Summer Ministry Team to District Youth Camps with students Reggie Dabbs, Mike Simpson, and Debbie (White) Hanson. She is presently the leadership development coordinator for the National Women's Ministries Department and is also a seminary student at AGTS studying for an M.A. in Theological Studies. She is a freelance writer/speaker and mother of three. She is also an adjunct instructor at Central Bible College where her husband Dan is on faculty, and she has served as assistant editor in the National Youth Department.

Doorknobs and Basketball

Rachelle Colegrove

Before coming to NCBC in the fall of 1982, I was driving home with my brother, Bill Wenig, after his graduation from NCBC in the spring of 1982. He said to me, "Make lots of friends and have fun because it goes quicker than you can imagine, and it's the best four years and the hardest four years of your life all wrapped in one." He was right; my time at NCBC flew by, and I made a lot of friends. I loved playing basketball – well, actually, mostly cheering loudly from the bench. I also played softball.

I enjoyed chapels and had some life changing experiences at the altar. One time when I was struggling with the call of God on my life,

Mona Shields, my Spanish teacher, gave me some advice that changed my life. The Elementary Education degree was just being organized, and I couldn't decide if that was for me or not. She felt it was a wonderful skill to have as a missionary if that was God's calling on my life. So I changed majors going into my junior year and was in the first graduating class of the Elementary Education program. Those classes were the best because of the close relationships built with your fellow student teachers and classmates.

I have used my degree to teach one year, serve as a Christian school principal for five years, and work as a substitute teacher in both Wisconsin and Iowa. Now, more importantly, I teach my own children, Donovan, 12, and Devon, 10, at home.

Mostly I remember getting very little sleep, working hard on classes, and holding down a job. The best gift I received while at NCBC was my husband, Greg. He is so perfect for me, and we are still madly in love after 19 years of marriage. God has been faithful while we have been youth pastors and then the senior pastors of two different churches.

Probably the most influential teacher for me was Larry Goodrich. He was the director of the Elementary Education program during the time I was there, and he was my basketball coach. He taught me to work hard and not to be a quitter – even though I thought I was going to die several times while running laps because I couldn't shoot a free throw to save my life.

I appreciated the fact that Larry rode the bus to NCBC so he could share Christ on the way to work. I do have one funny story to share about Larry. In the middle of the night we put up posters all over the school that said "Happy 50th Birthday, Larry Goodrich," and then we taped his doorknobs and doors shut to his offices. We convinced the security guards that it really was his birthday and not to take it all down. They believed us! Well, as fate would have it Larry was late getting off his bus because he fell asleep on the way into town that day. He had just a few minutes to get to his office and then on the platform for chapel. Needless to say people were stopping him to wish him Happy Birthday, and then he couldn't get in his office when he did get there. I think we ran extra laps in basketball practice that day, but it was definitely worth it.

Rachelle (Wenig) Colegrove is married to NCU graduate Greg Colegrove. They pastor the Assembly of God church in Corydon, Iowa.

Fit Together

Camille and Steve Lentz

As we look back on our years at North Central from 1983 to 1987, there are many highlights. Since both of us graduated from North Central, we decided to share our memories together in one piece for this history book. After all, it was at NCBC that we discovered each other and learned to "fit together." Let us explain.

Steve

One would think that growing up in an Assemblies of God home and church in the Twin Cities would doubtlessly have steered me toward attending North Central after high school. However, this was not a foregone conclusion. I remember hearing about North Central when I was younger and thinking that I would never attend "that school where they bounce off the walls and dance in the Spirit." After graduating from Apple Valley High School (AVHS), I chose to attend Bethel College in Arden Hills on a partial soccer scholarship and to major in business or journalism, while my good friend from AVHS, Sam Anderson, enrolled in North Central.

During my first semester at Bethel, I attended a Keith Green

A Faithful Past, A Shining Future

Memorial Concert in Minneapolis only months after Keith died in a tragic plane accident. During the concert, a previously taped concert was shown of Keith preaching passionately about the need to reach the lost overseas. I had recently re-committed my life to the Lord and was feeling that He was calling me to something bigger than myself. So during the whole meeting my excitement grew, and I knew that the call to missions was for me.

That night I went back to the dorm at Bethel and called Jeff Beaufoy, my pastor at Mt. Olivet AG in Apple Valley. I said, "Pastor, I feel like God is calling me to be a missionary. I need to go to Africa soon!" Pastor Beaufoy was excited for me but counseled me to get some training first. "Why don't you call Professor Jerry Falley at North Central? He's the head of the Missions department there." Knowing that the zeal of the call could wear down with time if not acted upon immediately, Brother Falley suggested I transfer to North Central in January. This is exactly what I did.

Camille

I grew up in an AG pastor's home in South Dakota and had heard of North Central Bible College numerous times through friends who were then enrolled, as well as through youth pastors and other pastors who were alumni of the college. During my senior year of high school I attended College Days and was very touched by the enthusiastic love that the students had for Jesus. Also that year I attended the Teen Talent competition which was held at the college. I was impressed with the atmosphere and was open to attend if God would lead me that way.

After high school graduation, however, I became an exchange student to Hamburg, Germany for one year. It was during that time that I sensed His direction to become a missionary to Muslims, partly because I had the opportunity to meet many Turkish and Iranian people there. So when I returned to the States, I chose to attend

Chapter Six

NCBC in the fall of 1984. The scholarships I had through my Teen Talent and Bible Quiz days were such a blessing. I felt the need to train as a teacher and missionary in order to get into sensitive countries, as I sensed the call to work among the Muslim people.

Overall, I remember classes that challenged me to work hard and organize my education. Great teachers I had that first year were Don Meyer for Pentateuch and Debbie Gill for New Testament Survey. They showed by their lives the importance of discipline in studying the Word of God. In the Missions department I was constantly stirred by the intense desire of Doug Lowenberg to strive for excellence in knowing Jesus and making Him known to others. The Falleys set the example of sincere and deep commitment to following the Great Commission. Their gentle spirits and warm kindnesses blessed me as they even had us students to their home. Bill Crew was also a remarkable teacher who discussed the Scriptures in ways that really made you think. Gordon Anderson has always won my respect, and I loved the classes I had with him. In philosophy, he covered the issues so thoroughly and caused me to think about man's thoughts throughout the centuries. I also remember his Hermeneutics helped me learn good methods of interpretation.

Additionally, I appreciated the opportunity to sing in the choir with Sandi Bradford as she helped us not only to sing our best but to sing our best for the Lord. Then, my time in chorale with Larry Bach meant so much to me. He taught us to strive for excellence in music while worshiping the Lord and ministering for Him. Both the spring and summer ministry trips were truly that time to use gifts God had given us to touch people both in the States and abroad. These academic and extra-curricular activities made such an impact on my life.

Steve

I remember one day going to my student mailbox during my second semester at NCBC. I found a brochure for Continental Bible

A Faithful Past, A Shining Future

College in Brussels, Belgium which Brother Falley had put there. I was confused as to the reason it was there but after going to Brother Falleys office to talk about it, I learned that he had chosen me to be the "guinea pig" to go as an exchange student for one semester to CBC in Belgium. What a joy it was to attend there and get my first cross-cultural experience, studying alongside 80 students from various nationalities. It was stretching, challenging, and a lot of fun. While there in the spring of 1984, I had my first taste of learning about Islam. Sobhi Malek taught a three-week intensive course on the subject while I was there, and the Lord used this first exposure to begin calling me to Muslims. One little side note about being at CBC in Brussels is that my Italian roommate took me out for my 20th birthday to eat breakfast in Belgium, lunch in Holland, and supper in France – all on the same day!

I have such great memories of the two short-term ministry trips that I was able to go on with Doug Lowenberg while I was attending NCBC. Doug was a true mentor as he showed us how to conduct ourselves and do ministry in a foreign setting. In the summer of 1985 I went to India for five weeks with five other students, and it was an opportunity to do a lot of open-air evangelism and preaching. This trip gave me confidence in the Lord and confirmed that being a missionary was His calling on my life. The Lord touched many lives through our team in a short time frame. The following summer only Doug and I and one other student went on a trip to Spain and Morocco for three weeks, working with Sobhi Malek. We learned more about ministry among Muslims as we needed to understand how to be led by the Holy Spirit in a sensitive setting. These trips helped to shape and confirm my calling and were a good foundation for where the Lord has me today!

One thing that stands out in my mind is the quality of professors I had during my years at NCBC. Specifically, Jerry Falley was like a spiritual father and guide during my years there. He helped me plan for my future as a missionary and encouraged me when the process seemed long and never-ending. He was an invaluable advisor to our student missions group, SCCAN (Students Communicating Christ to All Nations).

Doug Lowenberg had so much passion and a great balance of heart and mind as he challenged me in his classes to be all that the Lord had called me to be and not to settle for small pursuits. Larry Goodrich was such a great teacher also during my first couple of years at the school. His openness and honesty in class, sharing some of his struggles and weaknesses, was refreshing. He had an open door office policy giving students the opportunity to drop in and chat over a cup of coffee. I remember one time especially when I spent time with him sharing some family concerns that I had, and he counseled me with wisdom and fatherly advice.

Last but not least, Gordon Anderson was a teacher's teacher. Church History came alive when he taught it, and Hermeneutics was more than just a dry exercise in interpreting the Word. He truly loved teaching his subjects, and we students were all the richer for it. His book, *Orphans and Kings,* has been an inspiration throughout the years.

We so appreciated the chapel times and looked forward to them as a highlight in our days at NCBC. Worship times led by Larry Bach and Dave Pedde, tremendous speakers and preachers, worthwhile emphases such as the David Irwin Chair, and good times of prayer influenced our lives. And the special music on the Staff Appreciation Day, who could forget the song that John the Italian married student wrote for the staff, having been inspired in the middle of the night with the words "We appreciate you" which he and his band performed for what seemed like the whole chapel time.

Camille

Being a student at NCBC, I felt enriched by the relationships I was able to build with other students. Times on the dorm floor with the R.A., being with your roommates to share and pray, the Caring Connection with small groups, all these facilitated the way that we could bless each other as students. I remember Steve Wajda in my group, along with Leo and Marie Pier-Dominici. We had such good spiritual times and a lot of fun.

Steve

I have great memories of living on campus in the dorms during my first couple of years and then staying at the "Pi House" for men my last two years before marrying Camille. I lived in the Pi House with great friends like Jeff Snell, Tracy Rice, Steve Moser, Sam Anderson, Derrick Carr, and Lance Rensch. We had a lot of fun both goofing around and praying for hours in the basement. Jeff and I often got together to play guitar and sing John Michael Talbot songs. One notable memory is when the guys learned that Camille and I had gotten engaged. I was the third one that year to get engaged and in keeping with tradition, they gave me a surprise by pinning me down and writing "We're just friends" on my chest with a marker! This was the answer that I had given them for months when they asked about my relationship with Camille. To add insult to injury, they turned off the hot water when I jumped in the shower to wash it off. No hard feelings though; I would not trade the camaraderie for anything.

Both of us

We are forever thankful that we both attended NCBC and had the opportunity to meet each other. We both had missions classes together as well as common friends within the great group of missions students. We fondly remember the specific chapel teaching that Carolyn Tennant had in the fall of 1985, "Don't worry about the whole dating scene, just fit together with people." Therefore, we concentrated on the way God had brought us together as we actually began fitting together which eventually led to our marriage in the fall of 1986.

Chapter Six

One event that is the hallmark of our "fitting together" time was when we were both asked to share a testimony at the fall Partners for Progress banquet. Steve had revised the handbook for the student missions group, SCCAN, that summer, and somehow it had found its way to Dr. Don Meyer. After reading it, he called Steve to his office and asked if he would be willing to give a testimony at the Partners for Progress banquet. Dr. Meyer had also gotten to know Camille when he had traveled with the Chorale on the 1985 European tour through England, Belgium, Germany, and Poland. She had translated his sermons into German. Was Dr. Meyer doing some matchmaking? In the weeks that led up to the banquet we were expected to get together to practice our speeches with Roger Lane and encourage each other as we looked forward to the big evening when we became "partners for progress" in our relationship.

We are thankful for the ongoing relationship we have with NCU by hosting student missions teams from the school that have come to our country with Bob Brenneman. We pray that these students will be touched through their summer experiences as we were. Also, how special it has been for us to have speaking engagements in chapel and classes during our times on furlough. We look forward to what the future holds as we stay in touch with our alma mater.

Steve and Camille Lentz are presently missionaries in a sensitive Muslim country in Eurasia.

From Wide Angle Lens to Focus

Jean Johnson

On July 5, 1997 – one month before my actual departure for the mission field – I finished sealing our last box for shipment to

A Faithful Past, A Shining Future

Cambodia. Anticipation danced within me as I retired for the evening, thinking of my return to Cambodia for the second term. I could almost see the faces of Cambodian friends whose hearts and countenances had been changed by Jesus Christ. However, the following morning I woke up to these headlines: Cambodia's leaders battle for control (Associated Press). The article talked of a coup, a bloody mortar and rocket battle, injury and death in the capital city where I had resided for four years. I could feel my heart race. We all expected clashes within the coalition government, but we didn't foresee a large scale coup so soon.

My heart grieved, knowing that the Cambodians had already endured so much – the remnant of a previous gruesome genocide in which two to three million people had been systematically tortured and killed. I could not imagine the fear and panic that gripped their hearts with this new reign of violence.

God did encourage me with Paul's words in Philippians 1:12-20. I concluded that tragic circumstances can serve to advance the Gospel, and suffering can help the disciples of Christ to advance as well. Unexpected events often test our identity, purposes, willingness and motives in Christ. This whole incident caused me to reflect on the details of God's call on my life to serve in this small country in South East Asia.

God's hand on my life can be compared to that of a camera. It is as if my life was on the wide angle lens. God slowly turned that lens to focus on one object – His will. God opened me to His heart for the lost and the unreached country of Cambodia.

God first introduced me to Cambodia when I was a young girl not knowing the Lord Jesus Christ. Television programs soliciting funds for the starving children of the Killing Fields contained pictures of children which nudged my heart. The word "Cambodia" and the faces of the Cambodian children were etched in my mind from that day on.

As a teenager I was moving on the fringes of a relationship with

Chapter Six

the Lord. At that time many Cambodians had to flee death by escaping to the border country of Thailand where they resided in refugee camps, a dislocated people. Eventually, some of the Cambodians made their way to various countries to start a new life. My high school organized a program to receive Cambodian refugee youth into the school system. Upon their arrival, my classmates immediately began to tease these new students because of the obvious differences in language and culture. Yet, remembering those children's faces, I decided to befriend the South East Asian students. I wish I could proclaim to you that I instilled wonderful values and etiquette in the lives of my new friends. Actually, I taught them the avenues of ditching school in order to visit McDonald's instead of attending classes. My care for them was sincere, however, even though I eventually succumbed to the teasing of my peers and dropped those friendships.

God patiently introduced me to Cambodia for a third time as a student at North Central Bible College. After graduating from high school I was afraid to go to college. Nonetheless, I registered at several colleges. In fact initially I went to the orientation at a community college. As I sat there with fear and trembling, I decided to go to one of the other schools because their starting date was later. This would give me more time to delay the inevitable. I wish I could tell you that I chose North Central because of some heroic reason, but the bottom line is that it started later than all the other colleges.

Upon registering, I had no knowledge of the existence of the Assemblies of God, and I was determined to study at North Central Bible College for only one year, taking basic classes. I wanted to move on with my own agenda following that year. In addition, I resolved that the missions students who went to and fro in the same halls didn't know how to dress cool or match their socks. Thus, I had an aversion to missions. This sounds rather funny now that I am an ordained Assemblies of God Missionary.

Eventually, I was finally maturing in Christ that first year and posed a question to God. I recognized that I was becoming spiritually obese. I was receiving the Bible daily through classes and chapel, yet I had no outflow of ministry. I asked God if there was some ministry where I could volunteer my efforts and time. His answer to that question was immediate. The next day a classmate approached me with this request: "Jean, do you have any desire to help out with a youth group at Summit Assembly of God?" Of course, based on my previous prayer, I knew the answer without a doubt.

My classmate told me that the youth group consisted of South East Asians, primarily Cambodians. God gave me another chance! This particular time, I built relationships with their families and had more in mind than teaching them how to ditch school. (I actually went back to my high school to seek out my former South East Asian friends and invite them to Christ instead of McDonald's Restaurants.) As I visited these Summit families in their homes, God exposed me to animal sacrifices, witchcraft, idols, shrines and other animistic and Buddhist practices. These experiences sent me on an intense search for God's will in regards to His Great Commission. I asked the Lord, "Who is going to tell them about your great sacrifice, Jesus?" This path of searching led to five years of study at North Central and a degree in missions.

The person who impacted me the most was Jerry Falley. He was more than just a teacher; he was a mentor as well, meaning he went beyond classroom theory. He guided me and others to actually take action steps toward a long-term goal. That is why immediately after graduation I was already moving in with a Cambodian family and visiting churches to share the vision.

With graduation drawing near, God had placed a desire in my heart to go to Cambodia to share about Jesus, but this door was closed tight due to communism and civil war. I knew the Assemblies of God hadn't yet pursued this country and was leery about missions

Chapter Six

opportunities for single females. God instantly placed this concept in my heart: "Jean, you are not necessarily called to a place, but you are called to Me to serve a people." I gathered from this particular truth that God desired I start by serving among the Cambodians who had settled in the St. Paul/Minneapolis area.

I had learned from missions books that to know someone's language is to know their heart, and I determined to learn the Cambodian language so I could effectively minister. I had built a relationship with a Cambodian family of nine members living in a one bedroom house. I boldly asked if they would make room for a tenth person. From the generosity of their hearts, they allowed me to become a part of their family. We moved my bed and a few articles and clothes into the hallway.

Because Cambodian families are close knit, we spent ample time together. They patiently taught me to speak, read and write the Cambodian language. Each night I would stay up past midnight listening to their stories of life under the Khmer Rouge (a rebel group who committed an extermination of a generation of people second only to the genocide committed by the Nazis in World War II). It was as if this Cambodian family was turning a book page by page. I was quickly drawn into the pain and memories of this horrid event that occurred from 1975 to 1979.

I was able to build relationships with numerous families by practicing the language in the Cambodian neighborhoods. There was an apartment building in Minneapolis that had about 30 units with Cambodian families residing there. Due to the cold weather and their comfort with each other, they rarely made their way out into the community. I knew the only avenue to reach them was to move into one of those apartment units. I was the only extremely white person living among them. There began a first-hand course on cross cultural studies as well as the occasion to share Christ. I had the splendid opportunity to live among Cambodian communities and share the Gospel, disciple and church plant for six years.

In 1991, I received news that the leadership of Asia Pacific of the Assemblies of God made contact with specific government officials in Cambodia. Based on these events, the government of Cambodia for the first time invited the Assemblies of God into the country through creative access projects. I made application to the Division of Foreign Missions, and soon the long awaited dream that God had placed in my heart became a reality.

God has paved the way for the Assemblies of God and other faithful Christians from various ministries and denominations to share Christ through compassion ministries. There are no missionary visas available, and foreigners need a protocol with the government to be present in the country. Uniquely, God allowed me ample opportunity to develop and translate materials in the cultural context, evangelize, disciple, train and plant a church in the capital city of Phnom Penh. This church is called The Good News of Jesus Church which reflects its mission and burden for the lost.

After days of feeling out of touch during the 1997 tragedy in Cambodia and longing to hear news from the specific church God allowed me to plant, the phone rang about 11 p.m. The familiar voice of Srin, the church's Cambodian pastor, shared that they had been gathered for prayer and fasting when the fighting broke out. He said, "Jean, don't worry! God does hear the voices of the few righteous here that are calling out to Him."

Upon my return to Cambodia to serve another four-year term, I was blessed to see what God had done in the church. Presently they have been responsible for the church for approximately two years; I only attend upon special invitation. My role now is to mobilize, train and mentor this congregation as well as other Cambodian Christians, to evangelize, and to plant fellowships in unreached communities.

May God grant us singleness of action – action that moves swiftly and accurately according to the pulse of His desires and purposes.

Chapter Six

Whether single or married, male or female, young or old, may we all desire to have an undivided devotion to know Christ and make Him known.

Jean Johnson graduated from North Central in 1986. Upon graduation she served as a home missionary in Minneapolis and St. Paul among the Cambodian people until 1991. At that time she became a career Assemblies of God missionary located in Phnom Penh where she is presently serving.

Clueless But Willing

Wendy Beery

Common sense would have sent a country girl to a country college. It would have been logical to find a rural setting with cozy churches where I, with my limited talents, would have felt comfortable and appreciated. But God directed me to attend North Central Bible College where I studied Cross Cultural Ministries.

I felt lost, lost on campus, lost in the cafeteria, and lost in the chapel. The city of Minneapolis was both intimidating and enticing. I remember auditioning for choir and being rejected. I was devastated; I had been a soloist in my home church and thought I had a decent voice. It was an important lesson in learning how big God's kingdom is and how I can be secure in Jesus. Rejection is healthy for the soul if we can live through it.

A student body that was larger than my home town made for a lot of fun and interesting interactions. There were so many people who lived in such a small space, and we had to learn to live, study and play together. It was a great chance for me to adapt to an unfamiliar setting and find out what made me special. Just being in Minneapolis exposed me to more activity and noise than I had ever experienced. The poverty of the inner city shaped my burden and passion for those who are empty and lost.

Biology proved to be a good subject for me. It was in Dr. Sorbo's class that I met my future husband. Kevin wore a brown striped shirt, brown corduroys, and a brown bow-tie. I thought he looked like a cross between Einstein and Orville Redenbacher. But we became good friends and then discovered we wanted to spend the rest of our lives together. I honestly feel that even if I had never earned my degree, it would have been worth going to North Central just to meet Kevin. I am so thankful that God directed me to North Central and had my husband transfer from a secular university to North Central so we could get together. I knew shortly after we met that I would marry Kevin, but I didn't tell him that right away!

The Christmas break between my freshmen and sophomore year, I received a call from the Student Life office. Dr. Tennant, then the Vice President of Student Life, and Kim Lensert (now Wajda) who was then Dean of Women, asked if I would be an R.A. since one of the R.A.s was unable to continue through the second semester. This was one of the first times I felt North Central stretch me to be far more than I thought I could ever be. I really thought I was insufficient for the task, but I am so thankful for the incredible privilege of serving with some wonderful, godly women as an R.A. I remember so vividly our meetings in Kim's apartment. We prayed and shared, and I was transformed and challenged. Some of the women I served with are now missionaries, pastor's wives, and nationally-known speakers. When young women on my hall who had been abused confided in me, I felt God tell me that He was going to use my own painful history for His glory, beginning at that moment. When hall prayer meetings were sparsely attended, I learned that my faithfulness was what counted. North Central transformed my idea of leadership and servanthood.

Chapter Six

I remember receiving tragic news about a family member. I found an empty classroom in Miller Hall and collapsed on the floor. In just a few moments, a fellow R.A. came into the room and got me through the first few moments of shock and pain. I don't remember the words she spoke, but her heart was full of faith and compassion. I have followed her example when I have stood beside someone recently broadsided by tragedy. At North Central, I saw ministry lived and modeled in a way that has shaped me eternally.

Who would have known that Comp II would give me a heart attack? I enjoyed high school and did well in my studies, especially in English. I was thrilled when I tested out of Comp I, but when I walked out of our first hour of Comp II, I knew that I was headed for the academic guillotine. Leslie Crabtree had laid out the rules and requirements, and I was terrified. I knew that I would never be able to pass the course, and in the process, I would become the North Central poster child of failure for the class of 1989. But I knew I at least had to attempt to complete the course. So I worked hard and studied, took Tums to stave off the ulcers, and prayed for God's wisdom and extra grace on the part of Mrs. Crabtree. Imagine how I felt when she called me into her office. I knew that she was going to ban me from her class and possibly put me on academic probation! Instead, she told me she wanted to use my paper for her exams, which meant that I would receive a good grade, and I wouldn't have to take the final. I rejoiced and secretly smiled as my then-boyfriend, Kevin, had to take a test based on my paper.

Spring semester of my junior year I did a studies-abroad in Brussels, Belgium. It was another time when God blessed me with a chance to do something that I thought was a great honor, far beyond what I thought I was capable of. My future husband studied in Kenya at the same time. God taught us much about faith and trust in our time apart. Kevin became very ill and was hospitalized. I didn't hear from him for two weeks. Since this was before e-mail and inexpensive phone calls, I had to wait to learn what happened to him. Thankfully, he survived. I believe that God used my six months in Europe to birth a burden for the continent. It didn't hurt that I was eating fine Belgian chocolates while Kevin was eating food that has been described as wallpaper paste.

Transitions were overwhelming me my last semester at North Central. I decided to simplify my life by taking a job on campus. The one that was available which fit my schedule was cleaning bathrooms. I guess this was my chance to learn the importance of being faithful in the little things. I would go down to the bowels of Miller Hall and pick up my cleaning cart, take it up to the third floor, and work my way around the hall. I scrubbed the big old-fashioned tubs, dug grime out of shower stalls, and disinfected the toilets. God taught me the importance of faithfulness and practical servanthood. I learned I needed to do a good job no matter the task. This lesson has been invaluable to me on the mission field.

So what happened to this country girl who was thrown into the big city? I married the kindest, most godly man I know. We wanted to become missionaries right away but were turned down. We pastored a Deaf church in Fort Wayne, Indiana, learning sign language as we pastored. We watched God provide for us with miracles that allowed us to pay off our student loans, though we lived below poverty level. Then we became missionaries to Bulgaria, where we have served for 10 years. We wanted to work in a Bible college, since our time at North Central was so transformational. Our work at the Sofia Pentecostal Bible College is rewarding because we see people being transformed as we were at our alma mater.

There are several faculty members who deserve special mention. Dr. Gordon Anderson greatly impacted me because of his integrity and commitment to excellence in Pentecostal education and scholarship. He was a professor while we were at North Central and a missionary while we were missionaries, and he was always

Chapter Six

interested in who we were and what we were doing. I ruined Dianne's sweater when I sobbed on her shoulder at a conference in Budapest. I was feeling particularly discouraged, and the cry helped me immensely, though I doubt the sweater ever recovered!

I also want to mention Dr. Don Meyer. He has continued to be a good friend, and his Pentateuch class was a very challenging and fulfilling one for me, one that has shaped my life. His preaching and teaching flow out of who he is, a man of integrity and character.

Dr. Carolyn Tennant was and is an exceptional role model for many. While I was at North Central, I treasured the opportunities to talk with her. She is a godly, gifted woman who does so many things well. Many of us as students and graduates rise up and call her blessed. She has poured into many lives, and her example has challenged me to reach high and strive for excellence in whatever I am doing.

Our love and respect for North Central continues. We have been honored to be invited back to teach and preach in chapel a few times, and these were definite highlights in our ministry experience. We are thrilled that the legacy which began 75 years ago and has impacted our lives is continuing to change the world.

Wendy (Kristoff) Beery and her husband Kevin both graduated from North Central in 1989. While at North Central, Wendy served as a Resident Advisor and was a member of SCCAN (Students Communicating Christ to All Nations), the school's missions organization. Wendy presently serves as a columnist for the marriage and family column in the national Evangelical Newspaper in Bulgaria. She has been an AG missionary to Bulgaria since 1992 where she and her husband direct the Sofia Pentecostal Bible College. Before this they were pastors at First Assembly of God Deaf Chapel in Fort Wayne, Indiana from 1989 to 1992.

Faithful

Krista Herrera

When I came to North Central for the first time, I may have been a young adult physically, but I was a baby spiritually. I had accepted the Lord five months before entering the doors of Miller Hall and was unsure of what to expect from a Bible college or its inhabitants, but I did know that it was the Lord who had led me there.

Despite floundering at times as I took those first baby steps in my spiritual journey with the Lord, I was met at North Central with love, patience and encouragement. There were many godly men and women who Jesus used to touch my life. My resident advisor, Kim Sharp, took much time to talk, pray, listen, and encourage me through my first year. She was a constant reminder of God's love, reminding me constantly that He found me precious in His sight and that He could accomplish anything through anyone with a willing heart.

Kim Wajda who was the Dean of Women during my years, kept me accountable and was used many times as God's mouthpiece to deliver messages I couldn't yet discern on my own. She allowed me to be real, and she herself was transparent with me, sharing not only her struggles but also a godly example of dealing with them.

Carolyn Tennant also was a big influence on my life. She invited students to be a part of a prayer group that met weekly where we could experiment in the gifts of the Spirit and learn to pray more effectively. Upon graduation I became part of a team that planted a church in inner city Chicago. Dr. Tennant was an encouragement not only in word but in action as she mentored us. She was an example of the sacrifice of our own desires in order to be able to really pour ourselves into others' lives.

The majority of my most memorable times were spent in the

Chapter Six

Lindquist Chapel or in the Virginia Turner Prayer Chapel located in Miller Hall. I loved the Praise Gathering on Wednesday nights and remember one in particular where there was such a freedom in the spirit that many danced with joy before the Lord. Other times were quieter but no less powerful as we prayed together with friends and alone.

There were also many spontaneous prayer meetings that sprung up when needed. One night a student was missing so many students began interceding on her behalf. It turned out she has been abducted, and God miraculously delivered her that night from death when He directed the man who had abducted her from a church parking lot, tied her up and began cutting her ankles to all of a sudden take her to a hospital and leave her there.

It was at North Central that I learned to hear God's voice. I learned that when a sheep continually wanders from the shepherd that he would sometimes have to break the left leg of the sheep. This was not to hurt or to "teach the sheep a lesson" but for its own protection. It was done so that the animal would learn to depend on the shepherd and learn his voice and trust him. While the sheep's leg was mending, the shepherd would have to carry it on his shoulders and provide everything personally for its sustenance. For me as a sophomore, I felt the Lord leading me to abstain from dating for six months so that I could learn to hear His voice and depend on Him without distractions. This time was often lonely in the beginning as I listened to friends talk about their relationships or watched them go out while I stayed home, but as I spent time with Him, I learned to see Jesus as my lover and hear His voice for myself.

I now consider it a joy and a privilege not only to be a graduate of NCU, but also to work here. I worked in student accounts and now as the administrative assistant for the Academic Dean. Although my role may not be seen as an especially spiritual one, I come into contact with students on a daily basis, all of whom have needs not only related to money or academics but to Jesus. They need a sister in the Lord to respond to those needs accordingly. My belief is that of North Central's, that we are all ministers of the gospel, whether we are preaching it from a pulpit or sharing the good news as we go about our business. My prayer is that whatever capacity I work in, I will be faithful to my job and my calling.

Krista (Textrum) Herrera graduated from NCBC in 1991 and has been working as a staff member while her husband attends the university. She planted a church in Chicago from 1991-1993, served in youth ministry there until 2000, then was in youth ministry in Florida, New York and Ohio before coming to NCU. Krista was in the choir and was a mentor and peer facilitator while at NCU as a student.

Favorite Years

Stacy Sikorski

Although I love and enjoy my current life journey, my favorite years of my life were the four years I spent at North Central University (1994-1998). I always knew from a very young age that I would go to school at North Central. I remember move-in day my freshman year. I was so excited and did not mind waiting in long lines in the gym to register or the extra long line up in Room 203 for the financial work to be finished. Many of you will remember that, but for me at the time, it was all fun. I thought it was so cool that Vice President Dr. Meyers, helped me carry all my stuff up to my room. There weren't very many carts and the elevator was slow. That was the beginning of four of the most life changing and fun years of my life.

I was instantly hooked on all the great activities that the student life department and my awesome R.A., Yvonne Ozerities, had

Chapter Six

planned for those first few weeks of school, and I determined in my heart that I wanted to be a part of Student Life. That first year at school I signed up to be a discipleship leader (DL), went through the leadership class, and came back my sophomore year as DL up on 5 South. The leadership team up on that floor was amazing. To this day I am still best friends with the other two DLs and our RA. We just had a blast with our brother and sister floors.

Kim Wajda and Pete Drake (the Deans) were leaving that summer (1996) and so deciding to be an RA for a new team was scary but wonderful at the same time. We got the best of both worlds. We got the years of experience and knowledge from the former deans and the new insight and ideas from the new deans that next fall (Wendy Wirtz and Mark Chaplin.) For my junior year and senior year I was the Resident Advisor on 3 North which at the time was the second largest floor in the school with 52 women. It was a challenge, but I learned things about myself and about leadership that I still use to this day. Both years I had the two greatest brother RA.s, Jason Bachman and Brandon Diehl, and we had an absolute blast developing our floors into a family. Some of the most memorable highlights of that family were as follows:

At the Twins game, 3 North looked up and our brother floor had bought a few seconds of the billboard to tell us that they loved us.

My brother floor would go and pick up the sisters who worked downtown so that they wouldn't have to walk home. My brother floor bought a cartoon in the school newspaper to tell us that they loved us.

The wing council planned a floor wide birthday party, and we wrote letters to every student's parents asking them to send a small gift from them so that we could celebrate everyone's birthdays. We got gifts from parents that were missionaries overseas and foreign exchange student's parents as well as parents in Minnesota. It was an awesome night.

One evening I looked out my window and my brother RA had written in the snow that I was a "#1 RA."

A Faithful Past, A Shining Future

At Christmas time our brothers came in with a vase full of flowers and gave a flower to each sister along with a Christmas song and best wishes.

I could go on and on with wonderful memories of my days as an RA. They were truly some of the greatest times of my life. I still use some of the activity ideas in different groups that I have led since my NCU days. Being an RA and being a part of the student life department was a phenomenal experience for me. Any time a student at North Central can be a part of a leadership opportunity at the school it will provide them with extra skills and talents needed for real world experiences.

My closest friends that I have to date all came from my days at NCU. North Central provided a means of getting to know talented, fun and spiritually grounded men and women from around the world. My friends and I are spread all across the country and some are overseas, but we still stay connected. Our foundation was our years at NCU, but our friendships have grown and developed over the years.

Some of my sweetest spiritual memories in my life also took place at North Central. I was a part of Dr. Tennant's intercessory prayer group and had wonderful times in her office praying for others and for the spiritual atmosphere at North Central. At certain times it was quiet and we just basked in the presence of the Lord, and there were other times where deep groaning and intercession was needed.

North Central really went through a deep spiritual awakening during my years there. Some chapel and prayer services would last hours. I remember spontaneous services starting up in the chapel or on the floors. It was powerful. I remember one service where students started leaving and going up to their rooms and bringing down items such as movies, TVs, magazines, jewelry, and all kinds of things that they needed to get rid of that were idols before God. It was such a powerful time. My favorite memory was a night where we

Chapter Six

were having communion in the chapel. There were hundreds of candles all over the stage and as many that could fit on the stage sat amongst the candles and took part in communion together as a family. It was moving.

God physically touched my life at North Central my junior year there. About five years before that I had been in an accident while at youth Camp. The cartilage around my spinal column had been smashed, and I was always in pain. I went to chiropractors to alleviate the pain, but it never went away. I had been prayed over countless times but never received a healing. One night at a service in the chapel Dr. Tennant asked students to come forward if they needed a healing. I went up and just felt like this night was going to be different. I was basking in God's presence and with no one touching or praying for me, I was slain in the Spirit and when I awoke and got up, I noticed the pain was gone and to this day have never had that back pain again. God is good. Although I don't always understand His timing, He is faithful.

Several people really impacted me. Kim Wajda invested time in me, and I got a lot of one on one time with her since I was her on-call babysitter for Amariah. I loved her honesty and realness in her approach to life. Mike Nosser really helped me through a dark time in my junior year. Through his counseling and listening to me, I was able to gain insights about myself I had never seen before. Ten years later he and his wife Tiffany did our pre-marital counseling.

Dr. Tennant really helped me discover my true calling into urban ministries. I'll never forget sitting in her office on her leather couch crying about the city and my heart for the city. She looked at me and said, "Duh, don't you think it's because God wants you in the city?" I immediately changed my major from Nursing to Urban Ministries. That conversation completely turned my life and future around.

I was a student who didn't really want to leave North Central. I loved dorm life and stayed in the dorms all four years. I loved being around my friends and students and really enjoyed my student life experience. I loved the classes and the teachers and the chapel services. It was hard to leave, but I knew I needed to implement what I had learned into a new chapter of my life. I was fortunate to be able to return to North Central in 2000 as an adjunct professor after completing my master's degree. Over the course of the next three years I taught Intro to Sociology, Teen Challenge Practicum, and Urban Seminar (we went to Chicago and New York.) It was great being able to come back to North Central to give back to the school that had so impacted my own life.

One little side fun note is that I met my husband Adam Sikorski when I came back to teach at the school. So North Central not only gave me my education and leadership skills but also a husband.

Stacy (Grogan) Sikorski is married to NCU graduate (2003) Adam Sikorski, and they recently had a little girl, Reghan Jean. Stacey received her master's degree in sociology at the University of Illinois, Champaign, where she served in the office of minority affairs. She worked as a case manager in the southside office of concerns in Peoria, and then as administrator for Teen Challenge in Peoria/Decatur and dean of women at Minneapolis Teen Challenge. She was the principal of Chicago Christian Academic in Chicago, IL where Adam worked on pastoral staff, and now they are serving as college and young adult pastors in Normal, Illinois.

An SUV, an Accident, and an Evangelist's Call

Chris Mancl

I was so excited when I came to North Central University in January of 2000. Having been saved for only a year and half, I had such a hunger for more of God. I knew that God had put a calling

Chapter Six

on my life to full time ministry, but I was still confused about the specifics of that call.

My first year at North Central was a year of intense discipleship. God stretched me in ways that would forever change my life. I lived on the fourth floor of Carlson Hall in a room with five other guys, a situation which proved to be a challenge for us all.

I will never forget my discipleship leader that year who had such an impact on me simply by the life he displayed. I lived in the room right next to the prayer room, and every night I could hear him in the prayer room as I was going to sleep. I remember thinking, "I want to learn to pray like that." Ricky Spindler has become one of my very good friends to this day and has challenged me both in school and in ministry.

Being in classes like Life of Prayer, Global Perspectives and New Testament Survey made my freshman year a period of intense growth in my spiritual walk with God. I will never forget the prayer meetings that we used to have on our floor at least twice a week. Almost the entire floor would cram into that tiny prayer room. We didn't care about the room or the smell when you got that many guys in such a small area; we just went after God with everything in our guts.

During my freshman year there were a couple of radical guys who would go street witnessing downtown every Friday night, and they would always try to talk me into it. I grew up in a small town and was a little skeptical of street witnessing. However, one night I decided that I could do anything once and so I would give it a try. A group of about 10 of us got on a bus and headed down to Hennepin Avenue in downtown Minneapolis. I was witnessing with a girl who had never done anything like this either. We both walked around for about an hour thinking to ourselves, "Why are we out here again?" We witnessed to a couple of people, but it didn't go that well. Then I will never forget what happened.

We were standing on the corner of a busy intersection, waiting for the rest of our team to meet up with us. I was watching this guy across the street. He began to cross the intersection; then I heard someone scream and saw a black SUV drive through the intersection and hit that man in the road. His body flew up and over the car, and he had to be dead. The rest of our team began to pray as police and paramedics arrived. I was so shaken, all I could do was weep. When I got back to school, I began to pack up my stuff. I called my parents and was ready to leave. It was at that moment that God spoke to me. God asked me if that man knew Jesus. I had no idea. God said to me, "Chris, life really is not as long as people think it is." This was where I began to realize the call of God on my life to be an evangelist.

I returned to North Central for my second year, where God solidified many of the things that had happened in my life during my freshman year. I began to get heavily involved in ministry in the church and on the streets every week. I also went on a missions trip to China that had a radical impact on my life.

In the next three years of my time at North Central there were many incredible experiences that molded and shaped my character and personality into the person that I am today. I can truly say that I am who I am today because of the impact that North Central University had on my life.

I got involved in many different aspects of student leadership. I was a discipleship leader for a year and also a resident advisor. I will never forget being a discipleship leader in Mensing Hall my junior year. This year was incredible for many reasons. I learned so much about serving leaders that year. I went out of my way to be a servant for my R.A. I knew my place was to serve him and help him in any way I could. Organizing prayer meetings and Bible studies was a challenging new experience for me. During my year as a discipleship leader I also met the girl who would become my wife. Tracie was on my sister floor that year. It took me two whole months to remember her name, but once we got past that, we became very good friends.

Chapter Six

I will never forget when I became a Resident Advisor. One day at the beginning of the year I decided to play a little game that would teach all of the guys on my floor trust. We started in one of the classrooms in Miller Hall. I blindfolded everyone on the floor, and they all had to link arms and let me lead them all the way back to the first floor of Phillipps Hall. The point was for them to trust me enough to lead them throughout the year. When we were half way there I decided that we were going to run the rest of the way. While we were coming around the corner the last guy in line took the corner too wide and ran head first into the wall. He had the biggest welt on his forehead for the next week. Hopefully I was a better spiritual leader.

I have so many stories from my time and experiences at North Central, but what changed my life in the most radical ways were the chapel services or the times in the prayer rooms, weeping for the lost and seeking God's will for my life. I will never forget the periods of connecting with God in chapel. I loved hearing some of the best preachers in the nation every week. There are times even today when I will go back to those days and pop in a sermon tape from a chapel that highly impacted my life. Listening to preachers like Ernie Moen, Jon and Joel Stocker, Sy Rogers, Pastor Gary Grogan, and hearing Dr. Gordon Anderson on a weekly basis were highlights of my NCU experience. I will never forget the many times spent in the prayer rooms at NCU. These are places I connected with God in such a deep way. I heard God's voice for His calling on my life and for direction for the future. I received comfort in the midst of trial and painful situations in life. North Central was a place in intense spiritual growth for me.

Two people who had the most influence on my life are Dr. Dave Nichols and Dr. Carolyn Tennant. I took "Life of Prayer" from Dr. Nichols and was forever changed by the impact of that class. His thoughts on prayer and fasting were enlightening and are things that

I have never forgotten. Even though I was not an English major, I thoroughly enjoyed class with Dr. T. because she was always inspirational and challenged me. People thought I was crazy when I requested to have her grade my senior project on revivals, but I needed to be challenged, not just get a grade. I was on the team that accompanied her to Argentina as well.

As I have already said, I am who I am today because of my time at North Central. I am extremely grateful for all the faculty and staff who impacted my life there. Thank you for being faithful. I am very grateful not only for the education that I received while I was at NCU but also for the spiritual growth and character that occurred in my life. It was an incredible time that I will never forget.

Chris Mancl is a 2004 graduate of NCU along with his wife Tracie. He served as a Discipleship Leader, Resident Advisor, and caretaker of the apartments. Since graduation, Chris has served on the men's staff at Minnesota Teen Challenge, as a youth leader at Summit Assembly of God, and as an associate evangelist with Generation Now Ministries.

The Call

Dr. Donald Argue

When we answered the call to North Central Bible College, we knew it was God's will. President E. M. Clark actually invited us over a year before we accepted. His second invitation was confirmed by the Holy Spirit as God's direction.

We arrived at North Central to find a very discouraging situation. President Clark was a great leader, but faculty morale was low. Enrollment was not strong, and the neighborhood around North Central was deteriorating. If we could have known what we would

Chapter Six

face, the decision to leave the comforts of Evangel University, where I served as campus pastor, probably would not have been made.

God is so faithful! When we face challenges that we cannot control, we must depend on God alone.

During the summer of 1974, Youth With A Mission founder and president, Loren Cunningham, was in Minneapolis holding meetings. Loren and I have been friends for years. Together in prayer at about 2 a.m., the Holy Spirit began to reveal very direct promises regarding North Central. The first promise was that God's hand was upon North Central, and as we depended on Him, He would bless. Specifically, words of wisdom and prophecy regarding building an outstanding faculty and God's provision were given. The beginning ideas that developed into "Total Environment for Active Ministry" (TEAM) also became clear through prayer. TEAM became a foundation vision for the next 21 years. It was about 1) knowing God (the vertical), 2) discipling believers (the horizontal), and 3) reaching the world (going beyond ourselves to touch a hurting world). These concepts are based on John 13:34-35 and John 21:20-23 and when activated, God blesses his church, his college, his people. That's what happened for us.

After the intensive prayer sessions with Loren Cunningham, I was encouraged and energized. God had spoken! My optimism and faith was challenged when President Clark called at Christmas Break (1974) and shared that the most popular faculty member was leaving. I questioned the Lord in prayer and was assured by the Holy Spirit that this was in His plan.

The spring semester (1975) enrollment dropped to 401. Income and cash flow were not enough to operate. President Clark is a great man of faith. I learned so much from him. We both knew that God was our only source. Miracles of provision during those days are numerous, including building of the Frank J. Lindquist Chapel debt-free. President Clark is a churchman, not an educator. He is exactly

A Faithful Past, A Shining Future

what North Central needed in leadership at the time.

The following is a partial list of God's provision:

God gives gifts to His church in the leaders who are selected to serve. An outstanding team of leaders and faculty were brought together by the Holy Spirit. These included Dr. Don Meyer, Dr. Carolyn Tennant, Mrs. Cheryl Book, Dr. Gordon Anderson, and so many others.

Enrollment grew from 401 (spring 1975) to 1182 in the traditional baccalaureate program. An additional 400-plus students enrolled in the non-traditional G. Raymond Carlson Institute. North Central received the *Christianity Today* decade of growth award for the 1980's for being the fastest growing college of its kind in the nation.

With the rapid growth in enrollment, additional classrooms, student/resident rooms, and offices were needed, as well as qualified, experienced faculty. The biggest problem in adding new facilities was that we did not have the money. God miraculously provided in every way.

The college was in desperate need of an all-purpose College Life Center that would include additional classrooms, offices, an auditorium and gym.

Before construction was started, pledges to underwrite the building were received. However, we did not anticipate such inflation where interest rates soared to over 20 percent. As a result, well-intended people could not pay their pledges. The national economy was in trouble.

The College Life Center was about one-third completed when we ran out of money, and it appeared that construction would stop. We were desperate!

Flying back to Minneapolis from Washington DC, I felt directed by the Holy Spirit to Romans 7:14 "...but God who quickens the dead and calls those things that be not as though they were..." This word

Chapter Six

became a Rhema of faith, a Word from the Lord. I was scheduled to preach in chapel that morning. From the airport, I called the office asking that a basketball and two bricks from the construction site be placed in the pulpit. When I stood to speak, I sensed an anointing of faith. The verse from Romans 4:17 was shared with faculty and students, and there was a great anointing of faith. I took the two bricks and banged them together saying, "If you have eyes and ears of faith, you can see and hear the masons laying the bricks without missing a day." I then took the basketball and started bouncing it on the platform. Again, "If you have eyes and ears of faith, you can hear and see the activity in the desperately needed gym." At first the students and faculty looked puzzled. Then, the spirit of faith began to take hold, and all began to praise God for a completed building according to Romans 4:17. That chapel was incredible! We were out of money, and at the same time, praising God for the completed building. To God's glory, the building was completed on time and under budget and quickly paid for.

Then there was the miracle of the skyways. The cold winters in Minneapolis make skyways between buildings a necessary convenience. Contractor/Board member, Dick Vanman, encouraged the Board to proceed with the construction of skyways as steel had dropped in price. The Board voted unanimously to proceed. As President, this was great, but came with a huge problem – we didn't have any money. The construction was started and the steel delivered. Invoices had to be paid. This was a very low time for me as my faith was tested to the breaking point. I didn't know what to do.

The annual Partners For Progress banquet was held. I had little faith that the tremendous need to pay for the skyways would be supplied. Each Partners For Progress banquet provided an opportunity for people to give. Board member and Illinois District Superintendent Richard Dortch was to take the offering. Brother Dortch announced that a national ministry had sent a $100,000 check for the college. My faith jumped. Brother Dortch then said, "There is one provision. The $100,000 is a matching gift." We could keep what was raised in our banquet, i.e., if we raised $35,000, we could keep $35,000 of the $100,000 gift. My heart sank. We had never raised $100,000 at a Partners For Progress banquet. Brother Dortch led us in prayer and a miracle took place. A spirit of hilarious giving came over the people. In a few minutes, $113,000 was raised for a total of $213,000. The skyways were paid for in full. Praise the Lord!

God poured out His supply providing additional buildings in the neighborhood.

A fire caused by lightening destroyed the Photo Mechanical Services Building located behind the Lindquist Chapel at 14th and Chicago. Mr. Holsinger, the owner of the building, and I met for lunch. The property was appraised for over $400,000. I offered $100,000 and a donation tax receipt for the balance of the $300,000. This kind Catholic layperson accepted. Now I had another problem and opportunity for a miracle. We did not have $100,000.

The Minnesota District Minister's Institute was about to take place in Saint Cloud, Minnesota. The Minister's Institute was not a venue where funds would be raised for North Central. However, God had different plans. Pastor Dean Gross from Wilmar, Minnesota asked District Superintendent Herman Rohde for permission to speak and present the need. The result was a miracle. In just a few minutes, the pastors present committed $116,000, and the property was paid for in cash.

With the rapid growth in enrollment, additional housing for students was needed. I was in my office one day when a distinguished gentleman asked to see me. His name was Wallace Orfield, and he explained that he owned the apartments facing Chicago Avenue located behind Miller Hall.

The apartments and property were appraised at over $2,000,000.

Chapter Six

Mr. Orfield said he would sell them to North Central for $1,300,000 with a $300,000 down payment, and he would carry the balance as a mortgage contract. I saw an opportunity for another miracle, since we did not have $300,000.

Hours before the deadline to have the $300,000 deposited, we had no money. I received a call from Silas Liechty and his brother, Jonathan, from Jamestown, North Dakota. They had heard about the opportunity and need for $300,000. The Liechty brothers loaned the $300,000, and the apartments were purchased. Since that time, the Liechtys have given North Central far more than the $300,000 down payment. These good men were part of God's miracle.

Many other buildings were added during these years. They included what is now the Kingsriter Centre, Centennial Hall, Chicago Hall, the Elliot Condominiums, and the Zimmerman House.

Many other areas could be highlighted which include the addition of various majors, the growth of the Student Life department and its leadership development, and the growth of the supporting districts for the Board of Regents.

Spiritual Development

During these years, spiritual life on the campus was powerful. Daily 7 a.m. prayer meetings were started. A monthly all-night prayer meeting was held in Lindquist Chapel. Student outreaches involved hundreds of students each year.

As I look back on my 21 years, there are definite spiritual high points. One of those high points was a three day emphasis with Pastor Jack Hayford as speaker. The meetings were historic and, in my opinion, changed the spiritual direction and tone of North Central.

Conclusion

It was a great privilege to serve for twenty one years at North

Central. Thousands of people received training and grew in their walk with the Lord. Graduates are now reaching out to hurting people all over the world.

I am very grateful to the Lord for the privilege of serving at North Central. God's provision and supply always came just in time. Faithful partners joined in prayer, and people sacrificially gave to meet the needs.

TO GOD BE THE GLORY, GREAT THINGS HE HAS DONE!

Chapter Seven

Selected Photography

Presidents

The Rev. Frank J. Lindquist
North Central Bible Institute founder and first president, 1930-1961

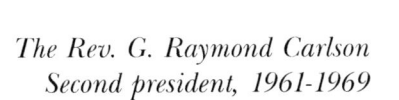

The Rev. G. Raymond Carlson
Second president, 1961-1969

A Faithful Past, A Shining Future

The Rev. Cyril Homer
Third president, 1969-1971

The Rev. E.M. Clark
Fourth president, 1971-1979

Dr. Donald Argue
Fifth president, 1979-1995

Dr. Gordon Anderson
Sixth president, 1995-current

Chapter Seven

Buildings

The Minneapolis Gospel Tabernacle, birthplace of North Central Bible Institute

NCBI's administration building, now known as Ivan O. Miller Hall.

The T.J. Jones Memorial Library, formerly the Tourtellotte Home

F.J. Lindquist Chapel
1973-2005

G. Raymond Carlson Hall

The Clark/Danielson
College Life Center

Orfield Apartments

Chapter Seven

Del Kingsriter Centre

Elliot East Condominiums

John P. Phillipps Hall

*Thomas E. Trask
Word and Worship Center*

A Faithful Past, A Shining Future

College Life

Students - 1937

Students - 1939

Chapel - 1942

Senior Skip Day - 1947

Chapter Seven

Classroom - 1952

Violin Class - 1950

Winter fun - 1967

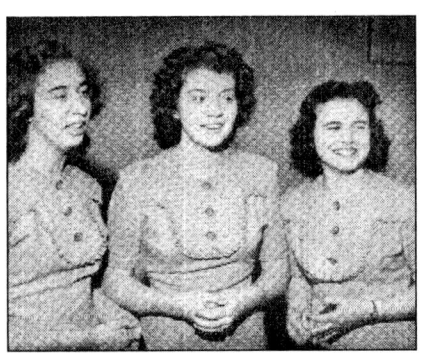

Women's Trio - 1964

189

Basketball game - 1971

Board of Regents - 1978

Accreditation ceremony - 1987

Christmas concert - 1984

Chapter Seven

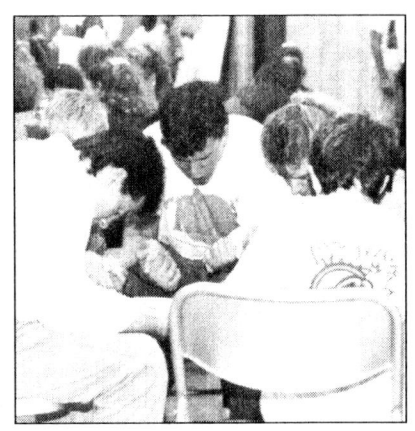

Students praying - 1990

Community Outreach Day - 1993

Students - 2003

Chapel worship - 2002

A Faithful Past, A Shining Future

Afterword

Where Is North Central University Going?

by President Gordon Anderson

North Central University has a great past and a promising future. Founded in 1930 in the basement of a church, a handful of students and a visionary pastor began a journey that has brought NCU through the various stages of being an institute, a college, and now a university. Properties in the Elliott Park neighborhood have been acquired, the student body has grown to over 1200, programs have been added, and the expanse of the present school would likely shock and please those who started the school 75 years ago.

But, what now? Where is NCU going? What does the future hold? The answer lies in a biblical picture that outlines Paul's vision of the church and also provides a vision of NCU's commitment to preparing students for life and ministry. In Ephesians 4 we read that God has placed a special call on each member of the Body of Christ (vs. 1, 4). Some are called to provide the five-fold leadership gifts (v. 11), and some are called to be saints and to provide ministry (v. 12). This is a thoroughly Pentecostal vision of the Church where the Spirit of God has been poured out on all flesh, allowing everyone to minister under the anointing of the Holy Spirit. These passages give a vision of the plan of God for the Body of Christ, the Church. They also provide a picture of NCU's future. Where is NCU going? We are going on to Ephesus!

A Faithful Past, A Shining Future

Most everyone would agree that the Ephesian model outlined by Paul is sound, but getting a school there, or a church, for that matter, is no easy task. Historically the Church has always tended to divide the "clergy" and the "laity" into 2 distinct categories, with the clergy doing most of the ministry and the laity paying tithe and participating in the services but doing little else. Martin Luther reformed this model with his understanding of the biblical picture of the priesthood of all believers, but there are constant forces that push the Church toward the bifurcation of clergy and laity that Luther so strongly opposed. The two most prominent forces are the professionalizing of the ministry and the secularizing of biblical principles.

These forces are at work in Pentecostal circles as well. While all Pentecostals have a theology of the power of the Spirit enabling each member in the Body for supernatural ministry, it is not always the case that all members of the church function according to the picture outlined in Ephesians 4 (leadership and laity in ministry), 1 Corinthians 12 (the gifts of the Spirit), and Romans 12 (another list of supernatural giftings).

Schools sponsored by church denominations face unique challenges in their efforts to promote the founding mission of the school and to maintain the spiritual vitality and biblical soundness envisioned by the founders. James Burtchaell, in his masterly work The Dying of the Light, outlines how schools lose their focus and end up disconnecting from the church that founded them and the principles that were laid out in the beginning.

I mention these issues to point out that we are quite aware that if North Central University is to arrive at Ephesus we will have to overcome the obstacles that lie in the way, obstacles that can provide ample reasons for a detour.

North Central University has a rich past that is part of the history of the development of Christian education. NCU began as a Bible

Afterword

Institute, became a Bible College, and then a University. These developments appear, on the surface, to mirror the developments of other schools and the history of the Bible College movement. The Bible college movement emerged at the beginning of the 20th century. Churches and denominations felt the need to prepare their lay people for life and service in the church and established schools to accomplish this. These schools, often called institutes, offered a 1 to 3 year course of study restricted to the Bible and Bible related subjects. The purpose was to prepare "gap-men" (D. L. Moody's term) for service in the church. This occurred at a time when professional clergy were educated in seminaries, following completion of a college degree. The Bible institutes were not designed to take the place of seminary training but were primarily to educate lay people for service in the church. These schools proved to be very popular however, and many of the graduates did enter full-time ministry.

In the late 1940's a number of Bible institute leaders formed what became the American Association of Bible Colleges (AABC) with the goal of providing standards and accreditation for participating members. This development occurred alongside interest in adding a fourth year of studies in general education so schools could be considered a college and be qualified to have its students receive financial aid. Over time Bible colleges began to offer more majors, some for preparation for ministry, and some for non-ministerial vocations. However, AABC maintained a commitment that its member schools would require all students to major in Bible, in addition to any other major.

As schools continued to develop, the liberal arts model emerged where emphasis on preparation for ministry and the requirement that all students take a major in Bible diminished, replaced by fuller liberal arts and professional track courses of study and majors.

These developments give rise to fundamental and important

questions. What are the differences between a Bible college, a Christian liberal arts college, and a secular liberal arts college or university? The answer that has emerged is that Christian liberal arts colleges offer a broader range of study in the liberal arts, but more importantly, they do not require a major in Bible. In fact, they may not require much study of the Bible at all. Currently, the Coalition of Christian Colleges and Universities (CCCU), has a standard that member schools require their students to take only three credits of Bible for graduation. If these trends continue, a secular school emerges to take the place of the Christian school founded at the beginning (Burtchaell).

These questions are important for NCU because the overall history of the development of schools reveals tendencies that NCU wants to avoid. For example, some say that a Bible college is a Bible institute on its way to becoming a liberal arts college or university, meaning that as these developments unfold the school loses it emphasis on the study of the Bible, on the preparation of people for ministry, and becomes increasingly secular. This is certainly not the path NCU is following.

North Central University, along with a few other schools, is pioneering a different approach to the historical development of Bible schools. Rather than adopt an "either/or" approach, where the school either emphasizes the preparation of ministers and includes a rigorous Bible study curriculum for all students, or shifting to a liberal arts model where emphasis on the preparation of ministers and the study of the Bible is diminished or dropped, NCU is pursuing a "both/and" approach, where emphasis on preparation for ministry and the study of the Bible is maintained along with a commitment to prepare students to be the people of God in the world functioning as Spirit-filled servants in the Body of Christ as they pursue degrees in non-church vocational areas. In this model, all students, including those preparing for vocational ministry and those

Afterword

pursuing non-church vocational majors, complete a major in Bible along with any other course of study they may choose. In addition, all students complete ministry requirements that are the same for both church and non-church vocational majors.

The critical component in NCU's vision of its educational mission is that all students are required to complete a major in Bible and fulfill ministry requirements. These requirements represent our commitment to a Pentecostal and Ephesian model where both leaders and laity are expected to be active in ministry and where the curriculum of the school supports that expectation.

So, where is North Central University going? We are going on to Ephesus and the picture of the Body of Christ outlined by Paul where gifted leaders (Ephesians 4.11) prepare spiritually gifted saints (Ephesians 4.12) to minister in a lost world. We see our educational mission as fulfilling the cry of Moses when he declared that he wished all God's people would be prophets (Numbers 11.29) and Joel where he announced that in the last days this would happen (Joel 2.28). We see our students emerging as the people of God presented by Peter as a unique company in the world, proclaiming the excellencies of Him who called them out of darkness into spiritual light (1 Peter 2.9), empowered by the Holy Spirit to be effective witnesses (Acts 1.8). We see the graduates of NCU replicating the ministries of the early church, whether as leaders with an anointing for ministry in the five-fold ministry gifts or as saints functioning with the power of the Holy Spirit seen in the lives of the two deacons, Stephen and Philip (Acts 6-7).

North Central University has a great heritage that is rooted in a Pentecostal vision of the Body of Christ. We believe that in the years to come we will see an even greater fulfillment of this vision in the educational mission of the school. It is a vision of the New Testament church, Ephesus serving as an early pattern of God's will for His Body.

On to Ephesus!

A Faithful Past, A Shining Future